Called To Intimacy

Called To Intimacy

Living In the Indwelling Presence

By George A. Maloney, S.J.

ALBA · HOUSE · NEW · YORK

SOCIETY OF ST. PAUL, 2187 VICTORY BLVD., STATEN ISLAND, NEW YORK 10314

Library of Congress Cataloging in Publication Data

Maloney, George, A., 1924—
  Called to intimacy.

  1. Spiritual life—Catholic authors. I. Title.
BX2350.2.M31477   1983   248.4'82   82-3782
ISBN 0-8189-0452-6

Imprimi Potest:
Vincent M. Cooke, S.J.
Provincial, New York Province

Designed, printed and bound in the United States of
America by the Fathers and Brothers of the
Society of St. Paul, 2187 Victory Boulevard,
Staten Island, New York 10314, as part of their
communications apostolate.

3 4 5 6 7 8 9 (Current Printing: first digit)

Dedication

To Cathy and Jim Kelly
who discovered God's intimacy
in their intimacy

Table of Contents

Table of Contents

Introduction

If God is love and we have been made by God for Him, then we have been made for love. But love is a call to intimacy. Deep down we feel a strong craving for intimacy. It is a primal desire not only to enter into communication with another spirit-being, to share ideas and ideals, but, above all, to enter into the deepest communion, a *union with*.

This desire to be united with another is a desire to be changed, or, better, to be transformed by the other's love into our true self that cannot be discovered except in loving union with another. Our lives are boring, empty and meaningless until we enter into a oneness with another.

Antoine de Saint Exupery in his classic, *The Little Prince*, beautifully expresses this loving transformation as a *taming*.

> "My life is very monotonous," he (the fox) said, "I hunt chickens; men hunt me. All the chickens are just alike, and all the men are just alike. And, in consequence, I am a little bored. But if you tame me, it will be as if the sun came to shine on my life. I shall know the sound of a step that will be different from all the others. Other steps send me hurrying back underneath the ground. Yours will call me, like music, out of my burrow. And then look: you see the grain-fields down yonder? I do not eat bread. Wheat is of no use to me. And that is sad. But you have hair that is the color of gold. Think how wonderful that will be when you have tamed me! The grain, which is also

golden, will bring me back the thought of you. And I shall love to listen to the wind in the wheat. . . . "

The fox gazed at the little prince, for a long time.

"Please—tame me!" he said. . .

"What must I do, to tame you?" asked the little prince. "You must be very patient," replied the fox. "First you will sit down at a little distance from me—like that—in the grass. I shall look at you out of the corner of my eye, and you will say nothing. Words are the source of misunderstandings. But you will sit a little closer to me every day . . . " (pp. 83-84).

THE GOOD NEWS

The Good News of Christianity is God's revelation that God calls us to intimacy. We can live for and with other human persons. But God's infinite goodness and love call us to share His happiness by living in Him. God's awesome transcendence, Christianity teaches, paradoxically makes Him *immanently* present within us in an incomprehensible but total way of self-giving to us.

God's uncreated energies of love penetrate every part of our being. They invade us most intimately so that in Him we live and move and have our being (Ac 17:28). God, as a triune community of Father, Son and Holy Spirit, lives within us in our deepest consciousness level that Scripture calls our *heart*. But the Good News is that God so loves us that we can become totally transformed into Him.

Jesus taught us during His earthly existence that He lives always *in* the Father and the Father lives *in* Him.

Do you not believe
that I am in the Father and the Father is in me?
The words I say to you I do not speak as from myself:

it is the Father, living in me, who is doing this work.
You must believe me when I say
that I am in the Father and the Father is in me . . . (Jn 14:10-11).

We, His disciples, are called to be *in* Jesus. The Father is pleased to see us living in His Son, loving Himself in His Son, doing all things to please Him in and through His Son, Jesus Christ.

On that day
you will understand that I am in my Father
and you in me and I in you (Jn 14:20).

If we do not make our home *in* Him, Jesus Christ, as He makes His home in us, then we will dry up as a branch unable to bring forth fruit.

Anyone who does not remain in me
is like a branch that has been thrown away:
    he withers . . .
If you remain in me,
and my words remain in you,
you may ask what you will
and you shall get it (Jn 15:6-7).

The reason why Jesus came on this earth and laid down His life for us in loving self-sacrifice was that we might be not only *in* Him but also be one with His Father. "May they all be one. Father, may they be one in us, as you are in me and I am in you . . . " (Jn 17:21).

A GROWING CONSCIOUSNESS

Jesus in His human consciousness had to grow in greater awareness at each moment of His earthly existence that He and the Father were one. He had to go to prayer and discover that the Father lived at the center of His being. He had to want passionately to do all things to please the Father as He gazed on the Father in loving surrender. He was able to surrender Himself to the Father's love to the degree that He became aware of the intimate presence of the indwelling Father in His Spirit of love.

So we are called to ever increasing consciousness of the indwelling community of God's family, the Father, Son and Spirit, within us. But the Gospel reveals to us that this is possible only through listening to the Word made flesh, Jesus Christ, who through His glorious resurrection now abides within us and is speaking His word to us at all times. St. Paul beautifully describes this growth process as the end of our human existence, the reason why God created us:

> Out of his infinite glory, may he give you the power through his Spirit for your hidden self to grow strong, so that Christ may live in your hearts through faith, and then, planted in love and built on love, you will with all the saints have strength to grasp the breadth and the length, the height and the depth; until, knowing the love of Christ, which is beyond all knowledge, you are filled with the utter fullness of God (Ep 3:16-19).

If Christ truly lives within us and is speaking His word from within our hearts, we are called to obey His commands through the power of the Spirit of love, for true love that unites two persons into one is measured by active self-surrender to the other in wishing to live each moment in loving service for the other. If anyone loves me he will keep my word, and my Father will love him, and we shall come to him and make our home with him (Jn 14:23).

As we dwell in Jesus, so we enter into a permanent in-dwelling in the Father and the Holy Spirit. But how can we grow in this awareness? Is it sheerly a gift from God? If the triune God dwells in all Christians, how is it that so few Christians show the joy and peace and ecstatic happiness that should be theirs in their consciousness of such a dignity? If God is totally present within us, He can do no more from His part in self-giving to us. How then can we increase our awareness of this indwelling presence?

Madeleine L'Engle in her book, *A Wind in the Door*, coins a new word to describe the inter-relationships between two spirits. She calls this activity *kything*. To *kythe* (this rhymes with the word *scythe*) is to make your true self present to another, to show your true self without any mask or disguise. In scriptural language it is a "heart" speaking to a "heart." It is a loving sharing of one's deepest level of being with another living on that same level that goes far beyond the mere communication of words or ideas. It takes place at the center or core of our inner being where love allows us to surrender in total gift and in total freedom to the other and the two become one.

Teilhard de Chardin described the strange alchemy of love when he wrote: "Love differentiates as it unites." True love always breaks down barriers and in ecstasy (from the Greek word, *ekstasis*, a standing outside of oneself) one moves not only toward but eventually *into* the other. Still more strangely the result is a quickening in great excitement of new-founded life and happiness as each person in the union with each other discovers now his or her own unique personhood.

OUR DIVINE CALL

This is not a "how-to-do-it" manual. It is a humble attempt to bring together insights from biblical and patristic writings as well as the writings of the great French philosopher, Gabriel Marcel, to present our Christian and human vocation as a continued calling given us by God from the depths of our being and from the context of our human situation to enter into intimacy with the triune God. As we live more consciously in God's presence and, therefore, seek to love God with our whole heart so that everything we think, do or say is permeated by the Spirit of love, we are also called outward to live in intimacy with others.

The beginning focus is on the intimate ecstasy that the community of God enjoys among its members, Father, Son and Spirit. We human beings have been called to share in God's ecstatic love. Jesus in His human consciousness shows us how He moved progressively into a oneness of love with His Father as measured by His inner abandonment out of love in complete obedience to please the Father. By his death and resurrection, Jesus is now a new presence made possible within the Christian. He released His Spirit who creates within our hearts, in the deepest consciousness of our being, an awareness of this presence of Father, Son and Spirit. This presence of the Trinity reaches its fullness of ecstatic self-giving in the Eucharist where we meet the trinitarian indwelling presence in the fullest symbol that effects in us what it symbolizes: divine transformation into God's triune life.

Increased consciousness of the indwelling presence of God comes as we turn within and live in faith, hope and love according to the inner Light that shines from within and dispels the darkness of our selfishness. As we push ourselves gently under the Spirit of love to listen to the inner Word of God and are vigorously attentive in discipline to uproot any hindrance to perfect surrender to obey the Word, we strive to live in loving abandonment at all times to the indwelling Voice of God.

The response to obeying God's Word is to strive to do all things in love. This calls us out under the impulsion of the indwelling Spirit to live in intimate presence to certain *Thou* friends. Marriage is not only the most common experience among the majority of human beings of such an intimate love in a stable, *I-Thou* commitment but it most perfectly reflects the model to which we are called in its depth of intimacy and commitment. The Spirit urges us out to love all beings in Christ and to use our talents in love to develop the happiness of others, especially the poorest in body, psyche and spirit needs.

The authentic test of how intimately we are living in God's presence is measured by how intimately we are ready to live for others. The transformation of ourselves into the oneness with God can come about only through a mutual transformation into other human beings whom we are lovingly privileged to serve. Our dignity and measure of sanctity or our life in God is shown by our striving to release God's loving presence in the world, but the world in which we find ourselves. For only in that time and space of our human situation with all its broken-ness and banality and even sordidness will we discover God's love as transforming all things into a sharing of Himself.

May this book be a call to deep, prayerful reflection in the heart and not only in the head, concerning your primary call by God in His creative love to share with you His very being in intimate union. May that intimate union disclose to you, in the words of Gabriel Marcel, that the *I* is the child of the *We*. And in that experience of your being swept up into the *We* of God's triune community of self-sacrificing persons who wish to share their very persons with you, may you be so transformed ever more and more each moment of your existence on earth and in heaven that you will allow your oneness in love with God to bring forth new communities of intimacy with those whom you meet on your journey through life. God is love and love is a call to intimacy. May you live in greater intimacy with God and in Him and with your neighbor and in your neighbor in the Body of Christ.

George A. Maloney, S.J.

Easter, 1982

Called To Intimacy

Chapter One

The Intimate Ecstasy of God

Some of the Greek Fathers, like Pseudo-Dionysius and St. Maximus the Confessor, were fond of describing God's love within the Trinity as *ecstasy*. In English, this word has many connotations that may distract us from the root meaning of this Greek word *ekstasis*.

Ecstasy is the element of God's love that describes His movement out of Himself. Love is a bursting out beyond barriers. It is a habitual "standing outside" of one's controlled and self-possessed being. It is a burning, driving force toward someone else to be gift to the other. It is a coming home and a finding of one's identity as a unique person in the loving surrender to another.

GOD IS A LOVING COMMUNITY

The great revelation Jesus came to give us was to tell us that God is one, as His Jewish ancestors valiantly maintained over the many false deities of their neighbors. But God is also a community or family of loving persons.

It is an ecstatic, loving intimacy of a Father emptying Himself into His Son through His Spirit of love. Such intimacy and self-emptying are returned by the Son gifting Himself back to the Father through the same Spirit. In the Trinity,

Jesus reveals to us the secret of life. Love is a call to receive one's *being* in the intimate self-surrendering of the other. In the ecstasy of "standing outside" of oneself and becoming available through the gift of love to live for the other, the Father and the Son and the Holy Spirit all come into their unique *being* as distinct yet united Persons.

The *I* is the child of the *We*. God as Trinity is the revelation that uniqueness of persons comes only from a family of two or more persons in love. In the very self-giving of the Father to the Son and the Son to the Father a third Person has His *being*. The Holy Spirit proceeds as the *Love* between the Father and the Son.

Christianity teaches us in the fundamental truth about the Trinity that at the heart of all reality or true *being* is the Spirit of Love that is calling two Persons into intimate "ecstatic" communion with each other. In joyful surrender the two discover their uniqueness in their oneness. Their presence to each other as gift, a giving away in free self-surrender of each to the other, paradoxically is a receiving of new life, new openness, that yearns still more to live as gift to the other.

Our faith assures us that such ecstatic love of the Trinity explodes out through the same Spirit of Love to be toward a created world. St. Irenaeus of the second century describes us human beings as "empty receptacles" to be filled by God's goodness. How exciting and yet how humbling to realize that we with the whole material creation are caught up into the trinitarian ecstasy of love. We are a part of God's joyful discovery of what it means to be uniquely a Father toward a Son in the Spirit of Love.

The presence of each Divine Person to each other is a similar presence to us. As the Father is turned toward the Son in total openness, availability, vulnerability unto complete self-emptying, so the Son is turned in the same Love, the Spirit, to the Father. That ecstatic "turning" to each other in love cannot be a different turning in love toward us. God has created us out of His ecstatic happiness that we might live also in *ecstasy*, in going out of ourselves and moving always in loving presence toward others.

Chapter Two

Created for Ecstasy

God is love (1 Jn 4:8). He creates us that we might share intimately in His loving gift of Himself. But this gift is a personalized gift whereby each Person, Father, Son and Spirit, gives Himself to us in a similar way as they relate to each other within the Divine Family. "Think of the love that the Father has lavished on us, by letting us be called God's children; and that is what we are" (1 Jn 3:1).

The vision that St. Paul has of our calling by God's predestination is indeed breath-taking, almost unbelievable:

Blessed be God the Father of our Lord Jesus Christ,
who has blessed us with all the spiritual blessings of heaven in
Christ.
Before the world was made, he chose us, chose us in Christ,
to be holy and spotless, and to live through love in his presence,
determining that we should become his adopted sons, through
Jesus Christ
for his own kind purposes,
to make us praise the glory of his grace,
his free gift to us in the Beloved,
in whom, through his blood, we gain our freedom, the forgiveness of our sins.
Such is the richness of the grace
which he has showered on us

in all wisdom and insight.
He has let us know the mystery of his purpose,
the hidden plan he so kindly made in Christ from the beginning
to act upon when the times had run their course to the end:
that he would bring everything together under Christ, as head,
everything in the heavens and everything on earth.
And it is in him that we were claimed as God's own,
chosen from the beginning,
under the predetermined plan of the one who guides all things
as he decides by his own will;
chosen to be,
for his greater glory,
the people who would put their hopes in Christ before he came
(Ep 1:3-12).

CHOSEN FOR HIS GLORY

God has freely chosen us that we might share in His glory. When God raised Jesus from the dead and "raised him high and gave him the name which is above all other names . . ." (Ph 2:9), His humanity was brought into a perfect oneness with His divinity and a new oneness with the triune life.

We, too, by God's goodness, have been made to share in the very life of the triune family. God has not created us merely to be "good" people who do good things in order to attain Heaven. He has created us to share in His ecstatic happiness. His uncreated energies of love permeate, invade, bombard us at all times as the three Divine Persons go "out of themselves" in order that we might "be able to share the divine nature" (2 P 1:4).

As human beings, we stand erect, among all other creatures, capable by God's gift of creating us according to His own image and likeness (Gn 1:26) to know God's personalized love for us and to return it. We are called by God to be aware of God's loving, gifting presence of Himself to us in intimate communion and to find our uniqueness and ecstatic happiness by becoming a loving, gifted presence to all whom we meet and serve.

Before we can *do* good things and become good people as God is good, we must experience our being in the consciousness of *being* loved infinitely by God. A tree cannot be urged by the fruit grower to bring forth good fruit unless the tree from roots to branches is a totally good tree in its being. Then good fruit will naturally come from that state of being a good tree.

How sad that Christian preachers stress so much a moralism of our doing good things with little or no emphasis placed on the unbelievable good news that we have been created to experience continually God's ecstatic happiness in His gift of Himself to us.

And it is only by faith that we can ever believe that God's nature, His state of *being*, is a state of His constant loving of us as He pursues us in order that we may share in His infinite beauty and happiness.

For God's foolishness is wiser than human wisdom and God's weakness is stronger than human strength (1 Cor 1:25).

AN EMPTYING LOVE

God's pursuing love for us, His readiness to forget and empty Himself completely in order to fill us with Himself as gift, is seen in His "pathetic" or suffering love, revealed and manifested to us in human terms in Jesus crucified. Nowhere has God's love reached a greater peak of fiery heat and self-giving to us than in the image of Jesus on the cross, totally broken, rejected and poured out for love of us.

We can whisper in shuddering faith, as St. Paul did, that He "loved me and sacrificed himself for my sake" (Gal 2:20).

Gazing upon Jesus on the cross, the image of the invisible God (Col 1:15), we know now something of "the breadth and the length, the height and the depth" (Ep 3:18) of the love of Christ and of the Trinity that will always be beyond all human knowledge (Ep 3:19). Now, in the experience of such infinite, ecstatic love of God for us, made manifest for us in the human form of the suffering and dying Jesus, we can be "filled with the utter fullness of God" (Ep 3:19).

A WAITING LOVE

Part of the ecstasy of God's love for us is not only His moving toward us in complete self-giving but is His vulnerability as He patiently waits for our response. "Love is always patient and kind; . . . it is always ready to excuse, to trust, to hope, and to endure whatever comes" (1 Cor 13:4-7).

God truly waits to be loved by us. Love can never be complete only in the giving. It is not enough that God be the Lover. He needs to be called by us our Beloved. The *I* of God is the child of the *we*. What awesome humility of God to love us and tie our happiness to His need for really receiving our love in return.

Jesus said: " . . . the Father himself loves you . . . " (Jn 16:27). God's love is availability to give love but He makes Himself humbly available also to receive in need our returned love. We have the power to complete God's ecstasy by calling Him into the state of *being* loved by us.

All this is a mystery and the work of the Spirit, who "reaches the depths of everything, even the depths of God" (1 Cor 2:11). This is the "hidden wisdom of God" (1 Cor 2:7) that St. Paul preached as wisdom of the spiritually matured. Such is a darkness of our own intellectual abilities and a light by faith to believe that God is not only ecstatically in love with you and me in His constant self-giving but He ecstatically waits for our return of love.

When you realize by the Spirit that God really wants your love and needs you to bring Him into His *being* your Father, your life changes. God's Spirit of love gives you an inner transformation of mind to experience what Jesus in His human life experienced. We, too, as Jesus did and with the risen Jesus living within us, can live according to the dignity to which God has called us, to live in ecstatic happiness as we go out of our selfishness to accept God's gift of Himself, but also as we seek "to act justly, to love tenderly and to walk humbly with your God." (Mi 6:8).

Chapter Three

Jesus in the Father's Presence

You surely have experienced the universal principle of human love that our potential to love is measured by the degree of love received. When I meet violent persons, criminals who have lived by attack and force, I see pathetic and broken people who invariably show the world their protest against not having received deep, unselfish love from parents or others. Their violence is saying: "I deserve to be loved. If you do not give it, I will take it by force!"

If you are good and capable of loving others, is it not because God's love transformed someone else into love for you? Loving people call us into transcendence of self-giving love to others through the love we receive from them.

Jesus came among us, as the Way, the Truth and the Life (Jn 14:6), to show us what we can become. He is the image and likeness of the Father (Col 1:15) but we have been created according to His likeness (Gn 1:26).

St. Irenaeus summarizes the scope of Jesus' incarnation:

> For this is why the Word of God is man, and this is why the Son of God became the Son of Man, that man might possess the Word, receive adoption and become the son of God.

AN ANDROGYNOUS GOD

Jesus is God's revelation in human form of the inner

nature of God. We have no way of knowing God, but through the Word made flesh, Jesus Christ, we can know the "inside" nature of God. As Jesus in his lifetime did works of power, miracles and healings out of love for the people He met as scattered sheep without a shepherd (Mt 9:36), so is the triune God the one who loves us by doing and by giving Himself to us.

But Jesus not only images God as *animus*, as the initiator who begins first to love us, but He shows us God as *anima*, as the one who waits expectantly for the return of our love. This Jesus does as the eternal image of God.

Yet Jesus in His humanity had to increase "in wisdom, in stature, and in favor with God and men" (Lk 2:52). He would grow day by day to manifest in human form God's nature as love until He reached the full expression in His death on Calvary. As He stretched out in greater consciousness to image His Father, so He offers Himself to us as the model for our human existence.

THE PRESENCE OF THE FATHER

Before Jesus could return love to His Father, He had to experience the Father's intimate love for Him. Before Jesus could be present to the Father in total self-abandonment, He had need of experiencing the Father's immediate and direct presence to Him at all times, in every event.

The Father bathed Jesus in His radiant love. The Father was present to Jesus in all His workings, in the soft blush of sunrise, in the wildness of the storm on the sea, in the smiling of babies, in the touch of a loved one. Jesus easily found the Father, inside of and lovingly acting in all creatures that came into His earthly experiences. That is the reason Jesus could profess to the Pharisees: "My Father goes on working . . . " (Jn 5:17).

JESUS PRESENT TO THE FATHER

Jesus at every moment felt the presence of the Father, both within Him and all around Him. Like a swelling ocean wave, the uncreated energies of the Father and His Spirit of love covered Him. Jesus thrilled at being the gift of that love. He knew experientially with every breath and heartbeat that everything He possessed and did came to Him from the Father's love.

> The Son can do nothing by himself;
> he can do only what he sees the Father doing:
> and whatever the Father does, the Son does too (Jn 5:19).

Every thought, word and deed were directed to the Father as love returned since He knew all came to Him from that Source. "And my word is not my own: it is the word of the one who sent me" (Jn 14:24).

SEEKING TO PLEASE THE FATHER

Each moment as Jesus walked in the Father's loving presence, He strove to become present in returned love by doing everything, not only to please the Father (Jn 8:29), but to do it with the Father. "My Father goes on working, and so do I" (Jn 5:17).

As Jesus in prayer discovered the Father and His loving Spirit deep within the core or at the center of His being, He sought to surrender the control of His life to His Father. Each moment brought Him into the *locus*, the place in which Jesus could lovingly abandon Himself in total gift to the Father.

He was the freest of all human beings as He progressively lived more intensely in the loving presence and gave Himself over to the magnificent, driving obsession in His earthly life to do not His own will but that of the Father. New bursts of love shot through His entire being as He ecstatically moved away from self-centeredness to Father-centeredness " . . . nevertheless, let your will be done, not mine" (Lk 22:42).

A PASSING OVER

Jesus knew that love was not a static gift of self, only given once to the Father. Love is a burning, consuming desire to become the other. Love of Jesus for His Father was a continued process of surrendering Himself in His desire to become more totally *one* with the Father.

During the Last Supper in the symbolic form of celebrating the Pass-Over, Jesus actuated that going out of Himself and into the being one with the Father. Yet His whole earthly life was a march over the desert of His heart as He passed over into greater union with the Father through the Spirit of love.

LOVE FOR OTHERS

As Jesus experiences the flood of His Father's infinite love covering His consciousness at every moment, His heart expands and moves out in loving service toward human persons around Him. "As the Father has loved me, so I have loved you" (Jn 15:9). The emptying by love of the Father who poured the fullness of His being into Him drove Jesus to loving service unto death for the entire human race.

"The Father loves me because I lay down my life in order to take it up again. No one takes it from me; I lay it down of my own free will . . . " (Jn 10:17-18). The love of the Father in the heart of Jesus had to explode outward toward others. Love begets more love. And yet such love in the humanity of Jesus needs concrete persons to actuate His great love for the Father. The resurrection is proof that He wishes to live intimately and immediately present to us in loving self-giving.

Chapter Four

A New Resurrectional Presence

There is nothing you and I fear so much as loneliness. We all know the feeling. No one seems to be close to us, loving and assuring us that we are worthwhile, even lovable. Before such loneliness we could easily yield to the dark fatalism that Jean-Paul Sartre expresses in his book *Nausea*: "I was thinking, that here we sit, all of us, eating and drinking, to preserve our precious existence and really there is nothing, nothing, absolutely no reason for existing."

Loneliness cuts us off from a community of loving people. Death is closely associated with loneliness since death tells of seeming separation also from loved ones, a departure on a journey that we fear will have to be made alone into uncertain darkness.

But the essential message of the Good News handed down from the first Christian community in Jerusalem which had experienced Jesus risen is that now God is present more intimately by the resurrection than He ever had been to mankind before. Jesus, God-man, who died for love of us to image the infinite love of the family of God, is not present to us as a resuscitated presence of the same historical Jesus of Nazareth in the same way as He was before His death.

Now everything is new! A new presence of immediacy to us has been brought about. Jesus risen lives within you and

nothing finite, no more loneliness, not even death, can ever
take you from His loving presence (Rm 8:35-39).

> Do not be afraid; it is I, *the First and the Last*;
> I am the Living One, I was dead and now I am to
> live for ever and ever, and I hold the keys of death
> and of the underworld (Rv 1:17-18).

A new time and a new space make it possible that we can
even now live beyond "sin and death" which Jesus has conquered by His new resurrectional presence.

> We were buried therefore with him by baptism
> into death, so that as Christ was raised from
> the dead by the glory of the Father, we too
> might walk in newness of life . . . For we know that
> Christ being raised from the dead will never die
> again; death no longer has dominion over him . . .
> So you also must consider yourselves dead to
> sin and alive to God in Christ Jesus (Rm 6:4,9,11).

A NEW SPACE

Jesus by His resurrectional presence invites you to enter
into a new time, the *kairos* or salvific *now* moment that transcends any limitations of your historical time which is under the
dominion of sin and death. Eternity is *now* yours as you surrender to the risen Lord Jesus, even though He still meets you in
the context of the brokenness of your historical *now* moment.

And He meets you in a new space. That space lies within
you in what Scripture calls the "heart." It is there in the spirit of
faith, hope and love that you experience your true self in being
"in Christ Jesus." In the space of your heart, in the deepest
reaches of your consciousness you encounter the risen Jesus in
the spaceless space of His healing love.

You receive eternal life in the space of your oneness with
the risen Lord. This new life in Christ has been yours in

Baptism. It grows each time you "put on Christ" by dying to selfishness and rising to a new oneness in Him. The Church becomes the "space" where you can encounter Jesus and grow into a greater oneness with Him risen in the sacraments, especially in the "breaking of the Bread." Here in the Eucharist do you meet the new presence of the risen Jesus that goes beyond His physical presence and yet is also spatially found within the confines of the materiality of bread and wine and the Christian community, the Body of Christ.

Jesus' risen presence is also present in His Word as it is preached within the Body, the Church. He becomes present in the teaching and guiding of the Church through its hierarchical authority with its charism to build up the Body in truth and love.

INDWELLING PRESENCE

But His indwelling presence within you, in the depths of your heart, is what makes it possible now for you to be present always to Him. Love grows most when there is immediacy. Now "by the game of the resurrection," in the words of Teilhard de Chardin, God has pitched His tent forever through the glorified humanity of Jesus risen.

The work of the risen Lord is to release within your heart His Spirit. The Spirit reveals to you continually that the Trinity of Father, Son and Holy Spirit dwells within you. "Didn't you realize that you were God's temple and that the Spirit of God was living among you? . . . the temple of God is sacred and you are that temple" (1 Cor 3:16-17). That Spirit is raising you to higher levels of awareness of God's intimate presence to you and, by pouring faith, hope and love into you, the Spirit makes it possible for you continually to be present to God at all times.

INNER LIGHT

The risen Lord floods you from within with His transfiguring light. As you learn to surrender to His resurrectional presence living within you, you grow daily into greater transformation and oneness with the Lord Jesus. You move away from the darkness of selfishness to the loving light of Christ who gradually permeates your body, soul and spirit relationships in all your thoughts, words and deeds.

As you allow Jesus risen to take over in your life and you are guided by His inner light, your thoughts become centered constantly upon God.

> Let your thoughts be on heavenly things, not on
> the things that are on the earth, because you
> have died, and now the life you have is hidden
> with Christ in God. But when Christ is revealed—
> and his is your life—you too will be revealed
> in all your glory with him (Col 3:2-4).

But you also are gifted by the Spirit of Jesus risen to discover the same indwelling light of Christ and His resurrectional presence shining "diaphanously" throughout the entire material creation. You are able to contemplate the physical world around you in the light of Christ's resurrectional power that raises up all things to a new sharing in His divine life.

BUILDING THE BODY OF CHRIST

To the degree that you are aware of being in the risen Christ, to that degree Jesus risen will begin to operate in and through you to extend His Kingdom, His reign of love, to other human beings.

> . . . Christ who is the head by whom the whole body
> is fitted and joined together, every joint adding its own strength
> (Ep 4:15-16).

Christ, the Head, is present to you by His filling activity. He is operating from within you with His infinite power, but quite dependent upon your readiness to allow His creative love to flow through you outwardly toward others. "Each one of us, however, has been given his own share of grace, given as Christ allotted it" (Ep 4:7). He lives in you and me in different and unique ways. He manifests these diverse activities through the charisms that His Spirit of love gives us. These charisms or gifts admit of innumerable types, but all are to aid in the building up of the Body of Christ that is Christ's Church. This is the teaching of St. Paul:

> There is a variety of gifts but always the same Spirit; there are all sorts of service to be done, but always to the same Lord; working in all sorts of different ways in different people, it is the same God who is working in all of them. The particular way in which the Spirit is given to each person is for a good purpose. One may have the gift of preaching with wisdom, given him by the same Spirit; and another the gift of faith, given by the same Spirit; another again the gift of healing, through this one Spirit; one, the power of miracles; another, prophecy; another the gift of recognizing spirits; another the gift of tongues and another the ability to interpret them. All these are the work of one and the same Spirit, who distributes different gifts to different people just as he chooses (1 Cor 12:4-11).

ONE GIFT

Would it not be more effective if you would understand your responsibilities to build up the Body of Christ in the light of your continued increase of consciousness of the abiding presence of the risen Jesus, living intimately and lovingly within you at all times? Instead of emphasizing what you may think are those specific charisms received by you as gifts of the Holy Spirit, you can concentrate on one gift, the most important charism of the Spirit, *love*, which you have received already in Baptism as the Spirit pours this love of the risen Jesus into your heart (Rm 5:5).

Then you will be able to see charisms not as static, already well-developed talents that God has given to you or has withheld from you, but as all your basic dispositions and aptitudes given you in your birth and throughout your life in your education and human development. What makes them charisms, capable of serving to build the Church, is that you cover them with the gift of love that is the first gift God gives you when you desire to live by His Spirit.

Then all that you think and do and say can be a charism because all is directed both by you and the Spirit in love. Then whatsoever you do to the least of human beings you do to Christ (Mt 25:40). In and through the resurrectional presence of Jesus Lord you are open to an infinite number of charisms since you now consciously possess the greatest of all gifts (1 Cor 13:13). Love comes in the realized intimacy and immediacy that come from your awareness that Jesus is truly risen and lives totally in His infinite power and love within you.

Chapter Five

The Holy Spirit Creates Presence

At the end of James Joyce's novel, *A Portrait of the Artist as a Young Man*, the hero writes in his diary:

Welcome, O life! I go to encounter for the millionth
time the reality of experience and to forge in the smithy
of my soul the uncreated conscience of my race.

Every event of each moment is a call for us to embrace that experience and hammer out a new level of consciousness, a sharing in the uncreated energies of God's love that surround and penetrate us at all times with His loving presence. It is the Holy Spirit of love inside of our every experience who calls us to the most creative force in all the world, the possibility of loving communion with others. And this call to creative union in love can be heard only in the context of our daily life with all its brokenness as well as its richness. Such "uncreated conscience of my race" can never be pinpointed to one encounter, be it Moses on Mount Sinai or Neil Armstrong walking on the moon. It is a continued call for every human being to accept God's Spirit of love in the context of this experienced moment.

It is the charism of creative prophets such as poets, artists, musicians and play-writers to be a "dew" line, to use the phrase of Marshall McLuhan, of what emerging "conscience" forces are coming forth from our modern culture. One predominant theme that constantly is recurring in artistic forms is that of alienation. T.S. Eliot writes: "We are alienated because humankind cannot bear much reality." Not only do we find all about us displaced persons, immigrants in mass movement from one country to another, but today we find the phenomenon of alienated persons, including ourselves to some extent, psychologically disintegrated and lacking harmony and meaningfulness to our lives. Spiritually we are estranged in a material world from a hidden God.

Discontented with our share of reality, we are continually evading the present world of experience and our own present humanity as the place, the "locus" where we will "encounter the reality of experience." L. Bernstein's *Mass* offers us this characterization of modern man resisting to be what he is:

> Give me a choice.
> I never had a choice.
> Or I would have been a simple tree.
> A barnacle in a silent sea.
>> Anything but what I must be.
>> A man.
>> A man.
>> A man!

The opposite of alienation is presence, intimacy toward others, an availability for communion. Heidegger called it a *mitsein*, a being with.

TOWARD COMMUNION

How pathetically we moderns stretch out reluctantly toward others to establish a community of loving, caring persons who can be the healing force in our lives of our loneliness and can call us into a joyful meaningfulness. In birth we are brought into an immediacy of primitive existence that is a communion not of our own choosing. As we develop through education and life's experiences, we discover the world of communication with objects. Persons and things are "over there" while we are "over here," separating ourselves from the others by our ability to put them into rational and impersonal boxes.

But all of us in the maturing of our lives receive calls from God's Spirit to leave the world of science and objects and to take the risk to enter into the world of mysterious presence in love toward another. It is a return to the intimacy of the Garden of Eden where in loving communion we can walk with God in the love we share with others.

GOD'S PRESENCE TO US

God becomes present to us in His Spirit of love. Love brings about communion. Self-defenses fall apart as love unites two persons into a oneness where before two objects looked at each other. We find new *being*, our true personhood, in the union of another.

The Spirit, as the Book of *Genesis* describes God's loving activity, has always been present in our material world. God's love hovers over the unformed chaos, the black potential, that waits to be called into being by the spark of unifying love. "Now the earth was a formless void, there was darkness over the deep, and God's spirit hovered over the water" (Gn 1:2).

When God created woman and gave her to man, He breathed His Spirit of intimate love into them and bound them together into a union, bone from his bones, and flesh from his flesh (Gn 2:23). God joined them together in love and they became "one body" (Gn 2:24) and no force in the world was to cut this union asunder.

God's Spirit is depicted as a wind and a breath, the *ruah*, that is God's presence as power, fresh, dynamic and moving the whole universe into harmony. This Spirit of intimate love is omnipresent. The heavens cannot control or contain this

Spirit (1 K 8:27). "Do I not fill heaven and earth?—it is Yahweh who speaks" (Jr 23:24).

> Where could I go to escape your spirit?
> Where could I flee from your presence?
> If I climb the heavens you are there,
> there too, if I lie in Sheol (Ps 139:7-8).

This Spirit of God is all-knowing. "Yahweh, you examine me and know me, you know if I am standing or sitting, you read my thoughts from far away, whether I walk or lie down, you are watching, you know every detail of my conduct" (Ps 139:1-3).

A LOVING PRESENCE AMONG HIS PEOPLE

God's loving Spirit brings God, not only near His people by His omnipresence in all things and His all-knowing probing understanding, but this Spirit forms community. God wishes to share His *being* with His chosen ones to whom He commits Himself with fidelity and protective love. "I will set up my dwelling among you and I will not cast you off. I will live in your midst; I will be your God and you shall be my people" (Lv 26:11-12). God forms his *hesed* covenantal love and pledges His continued fidelity (*emet*) to be always a God who has pitched His tent among His people.

> I will betroth you to myself forever,
> betroth you with integrity and justice,
> with tenderness and love;
> I will betroth you to myself with faithfulness,
> and you will come to know Yahweh (Ho 2:21-22).

Abraham J. Heschel presents Yahweh as a God who is a searching, involving God who participates in the historical experiences of His people.

> He is the father of all men, not only a judge; he is a lover engaged to his people, not only a king. God stands in a passion-

ate relationship to man. His love or anger, his mercy or disappointment is an expression of his profound participation in the history of Israel and all men.

This God of Abraham, Isaac and Jacob is a pursuing God who truly wants His chosen ones to love Him in return for His immense, burning love for them. Yahweh yearns for their surrendering love to Himself who has completely surrendered Himself to loving service in order that His people might share His happiness in intimate union. He carved His people's names "on the palms" of His hands (Is 49:16). Should a mother ever forget her sucking child, Yahweh would never forsake His people (Is 49:15).

I did forsake you for a brief moment,
but with great love will I take you back.
In excess of anger, for a moment
I hid my face from you.
But with everlasting love I have taken pity on you,
says Yahweh, your redeemer (Is 54:7-8).

EMMANUEL—GOD AMONG US

But it is when God's Word leapt forth from out of the bosom of the eternal Father and "pitched his tent among us" (Jn 1:14) that the Holy Spirit most manifests God's presence among His people. St. John the Evangelist climaxes the progressive dwelling of God in His powerful glory (*Shekinah*) among His people as he describes the Word enfleshed for us: ". . . and we saw his glory, the glory that is his as the only Son of the Father, full of grace and truth" (Jn 1:14).

Yahweh had stayed among His chosen people in the Ark of the Covenant and then in the Holy of Holies within the Temple of Mount Zion. Now God speaks His loving Word and pitches His tent or tabernacle and dwells among the newly chosen people of Israel in the person of Jesus of Nazareth.

This active Word of God, that was, from the beginning, creating new relationships with His people, through the power of the Spirit of love, now centers His presence in the "tent" of human flesh. The glory of God's divinity shone through the frailness and lowliness of His humanity. The glory or power of God's Spirit of love radiated in the teachings and miracles of this man, Jesus. As He touched the maimed and diseased around Him, His humanity became the point of encounter as once in the desert the tabernacle was, through which the life of God's loving presence could flow into the lives of all who accepted Him.

Jesus' release or sending of the Holy Spirit, whom He promised to give to His followers who believed in Him as the Son of God (Jn 16:7), would teach Christians all they needed to know about Him. That same Spirit of love would give them the power to become witnesses to the great, good news that Jesus and His heavenly Father live within them. Now the followers of Jesus can be led into the complete truth (Jn 16:7-15).

INDWELLING SPIRIT

As the Holy Spirit is the hidden, "kenotic" presence of love within the Trinity, so the same personalized love, binding the Father and the Son together into intimate communion, binds us into an intimate sharing of this same Father and Son. Jesus could pour out the fullness of the Holy Spirit of love only after He died, because only then could His followers understand the infinite love of the Father for His children as imaged in the dying Jesus.

The Spirit that the risen Jesus sends by asking His Father in glory is seen as the loving force of God Himself, divinizing all who are open to receive His Gift. This holiness given to us to transform us into heirs of God, true children of God (Rm 8:15; Gal 4:6), is the very indwelling of God's Spirit taking possession of us Christians, as He penetrates our mind, our thoughts, our actions with the very life of God.

This indwelling Spirit brings about a new regeneration. This new birth Jesus foretold to Nicodemus when He stressed the necessity of human beings being reborn of water and the Spirit (Jn 3:5-6). St. Paul never ceases to describe the main work of the Spirit as bringing us into a new life, a life in Jesus which regenerates us into true Children of God.

> . . . the Spirit of God has made his home in you . . . Though your body may be dead it is because of sin, but if Christ is in you then your spirit is life because you have been justified; and if the Spirit of him who raised Jesus from the dead is living in you, then he who raised Jesus from the dead will give life to your own mortal bodies through his Spirit living in you (Rm 8:9-11).

In this Spirit we experience God's most intimate presence living within us as in His temple. Such a loving presence so immediately experienced as an indwelling love, fills us with a new inner dignity touching all human relationships of body, soul and spirit.

> Didn't you realize that you were God's temple and that the Spirit of God was living among you? If anybody should destroy the temple of God, God will destroy him, because the temple of God is sacred; and you are that temple (1 Cor 3:16; cf. 1 Cor 6:19).

How can we Christians ever again be lonely in the experience of the indwelling Spirit who witnesses within us by His gifts of faith, hope and love that the Trinity dwells literally within us and loves us with an infinite love? Not only does the Spirit of Jesus and the Father bring about the new life of God, Father, Son and Spirit within us but He also fosters and brings this new life to its fullness in the proportion that we allow the Spirit to become normative in guiding us Christians to make choices according to the mind of Christ.

FREED TO LOVE

The presence of the Spirit leads us into a freedom from an extrinsic law. We yield more and more to His interior communication that we receive when we turn within and listen to the Spirit of Jesus. "If you are led by the Spirit, no law can touch you" (Gal 5:18).

The Spirit guides the Christian who lives interiorly to respond constantly to the living Word within him. The Spirit reveals to you God's will through the community of loving-persons with whom you gather to praise God. The Spirit builds you into a vibrant member of the Body of Christ as you surrender to accept and live by the Spirit's gift of love. You desire to use your talents and charisms in love to build up the Church.

The Spirit brings you into the peak of oneness with Christ in His Body as you are led by the Spirit to participate in the Holy Eucharist. The Spirit in the Eucharist brings together the perfect symbol and sign that effects what it symbolizes, the union of the one Spirit of Christ in the many members with all members seeking the unity of knowledge and holiness of a formed, unified community: the Church.

And we can be certain whether we are being guided by the Spirit of Jesus and listening to His Word by the fruit that accompanies our actions done in the Spirit of love.

> What the Spirit brings is very different: love, joy, peace, patience, kindness, goodness, trustfulness, gentleness and self-control. There can be no law against things like that, of course. You cannot belong to Christ Jesus unless you crucify all self-indulgent passions and desires. Since the Spirit is our life, let us be directed by the Spirit (Gal 5:22-25).

LOVE MAKES ALL THINGS POSSIBLE

This Spirit of the risen Jesus reveals to you how you are able to do always your actions to please God, to lead "a life acceptable to him in all its aspects" (Col. 1:10). But in order to put on the mind of Christ and live in love as Jesus commands us, you and I have need of the Spirit to live in the dialectic of cross and resurrection.

What is impossible for us to accept by way of suffering as a part of love given to others becomes possible as the Spirit fills us with the inner law of charity. It is by the Spirit's love infused into us that we can put to death the old "carnal" way of thinking and we can live habitually according to the mind of Jesus. Through the love of God's Spirit poured into our hearts (Rm 5:5), we can always be patient and kind, never jealous, or boastful or conceited or rude or selfish. We need no more to take offense or be resentful. We will always be ready to excuse, to trust, to hope and to endure whatever comes. For love is the greatest gift of God. It is truly the Holy Spirit Himself operating freely within us (1 Cor 13:3-13).

INTIMACY BEGETS INTIMACY

Through the Holy Spirit you are brought into the very intimacy of the Trinity. You are healed of your "low profile" of yourself as the Spirit assures you of your inner, transformed beauty through the gift of God's overwhelming, gratuitous gift of Himself to you in love. In such experienced love that is always present within you, you can find the power to contemplate yourself living each moment in the risen life of Jesus, present within you. This is the peak of the work of the Spirit, to lead you to intimacy and to freedom.

Now this Lord is the Spirit, and where the Spirit of the Lord is, there is freedom. And we, with our unveiled faces reflecting like

mirrors the brightness of the Lord, all grow brighter and brighter as we are turned into the image that we reflect, this is the
work of the Lord who is Spirit. (2 Cor 3:17-18).

Such intimacy given you by the Spirit allows you in the
new freedom that begets you into your authentic *I* to stretch
out as you offer yourself in loving service to be intimate to
others. The Spirit urges you outward, not only to discover
Jesus in others, but to labor incessantly to bring Him forth
more fully in them. God's intimate sharing of Himself with you
is not to end there. God's love is totally ordered to the individual that you are in God's Logos. But the total *you* in God's
plan is found also in the total Christ, made up of every individual, made to become a living member of His Body.

Intimacy with God begets intimacy, at least the desire that
we can become intimate within the Body of Christ with every
human being, created by God according to His own image that
is Christ (Gn 1:26; Col 1:16). The true test of how intimate you
are with God is found in your love and humble service toward
your neighbor. This is the work of the Spirit. St. Paul preached
this as the doctrine taught by Jesus Christ:

> Serve one another, rather, in words of love, since the whole
> of the Law is summarized in a single command;
> Love your neighbor as yourself (Gal 5:13-14).

Chapter Six

Eucharistic Presence

The recent film, *Chariots of Fire*, presents a moving drama of two runners who compete for Great Britain in the 1924 Olympics held in Paris. Both athletes train fiercely and compete against all challengers with a driving passion. The one hero, a Jewish Englishman, seeks to be number one out of a paranoia on behalf of his Jewish people. The other, Eric Liddell, is a Christian born in China of missionary parents. He runs in order to glorify God by surrendering to God's inner presence and power. He was aware that God ran with him, pouring into him super-human strength.

Christians, in union with the faith of the first disciples of Jesus, know that in the beautiful gift of Jesus Christ in the sacrament of the Eucharist they too possess a new presence and power of God abiding within them.

THE FULLNESS OF INTIMACY

Christ's eucharistic presence is not one of the many ways in which He becomes present to us. We can wrongly limit His presence in this unique manner of self-giving and totally misconstrue therefore the extent of His intimacy to us who receive Him in this sacrament of love if we objectivize the Eucharist as a form of presence in a "place" where Jesus is present in "this" host or inside of that tabernacle "over there."

All other presences of Jesus in our material world meet in the Eucharist and are transcended and superseded by this unique presence. It is the climax of God's self-giving to us and therefore contains all other forms of God's presence "toward" us. In the Eucharist, God literally gives us a part of His very being as we receive the Body and Blood of Jesus Christ. St. Cyril of Alexandria writes: "Fundamentally the Eucharist is a victory—a victory of one who is absent to become present in a world which conceals him."

Now we have the means whereby we can enter into the fullness of God's intimate sharing of His very own life with us through touching the glorified, risen humanity of Christ in the Eucharist. Not only is it the entire, historical Jesus of Nazareth that we receive, with all His earthly life of teaching, preaching, healing and performing miracles, the greatest of which is His passion and death on our behalf, but we receive the risen Lord of glory with the presence of the Blessed Trinity. In His humanity that by the resurrection has been raised to enter into the divine community of the Father, Son and Spirit, we have now the High-Priest who can intercede before the throne of God on our behalf.

> In other words, brothers, through the blood of Jesus we have the right to enter the sanctuary, by a new way which he has opened for us, a living opening through the curtain, that is to say, his body. And we have the supreme high priest over all the house of God. So as we go in, let us be sincere in heart and filled with faith, our minds sprinkled and free from any trace of bad conscience and our bodies washed with pure water. Let us keep firm in the hope we profess, because the one who made the promise is faithful. Let us be concerned for each other, to stir a response in love and good works (Heb 10:19-24).

A SHARING IN THE TRINITY

God's desire to become intimately present to you reaches the culmination of realization when He can share His being with you through the Eucharist. The Eucharist fulfills the reason why God's Word became flesh, namely, that we might share in God's very own life.

The mysteries of the Incarnation, the death and resurrection of Jesus, His ascension and outpouring of His Spirit reach fulfillment in the Eucharist as we are privileged beyond understanding to touch, not only the total Christ, God-Man, but through Him to enter into the very intimacy of touching the Father and the Holy Spirit. The glory that the Father gave Jesus in the resurrection was to raise His human nature into a oneness with the natural state of His being the only begotten Son of the Father from all eternity.

The basis for your living intimately in the presence of the triune God is found in the mystery of the Eucharist. Here is the climax of God's eternal plan when he "chose us in Christ, to be holy and spotless, and to live through love in his presence" (Ep 1:4). Sin had destroyed the likeness to Jesus Christ within us. It hindered the Holy Spirit from raising us to an awareness in grace that Jesus truly lives in us and we in Him. But the Eucharist (and here we see the need of preparation to receive worthily this sacrament through repentance and an authentic *metanoia* or conversion) restores and powerfully builds up this oneness with Christ.

It is the Holy Spirit in the Eucharist who brings us into the *koinonia* or fellowship with the Trinity. Through the intensification of our own union in a very physical way as we eat the Body and drink the Blood of Christ, the Spirit brings us into a new quickening of faith, hope and love to realize with new awareness our being also one with the Father and His Spirit.

This is the fulfillment of Christ's prayer in the Last Supper Discourse as found in St. John's Gospel.

> May they all be one,
> Father, may they be one in us,
> as you are in me and I am in you,
> so that the world may believe it was you who sent me.
> I have given them the glory you gave to me,
> that they may be one as we are one.
> With me in them and you in me,
> may they be so completely one
> that the world will realize that it was you who sent me
> and that I have loved them as much as you loved me
> (Jn 17:21-23).

St. Cyril of Alexandria clearly grasped that we are not only restored into the likeness of Jesus Christ in the Eucharist but we enter into a new oneness with the Father and the Holy Spirit.

> Accordingly we are all one in the Father and in the Son and in the Holy Spirit; one, I say, in unity of relationship of love and concord with God and one another . . . one by conformity in godliness, by communion in the sacred body of Christ, and by fellowship in the one and Holy Spirit and this is a real, physical union.

Receiving the total Christ we also receive the total Father and Holy Spirit, for in the intimacy of the family of God no person can be separated from the other two. If Jesus and the Father abide in each other and have come to abide within us in the Eucharist (Jn 14:23), the Holy Spirit, as the bond of unity that brings them together and who proceeds as love from their abiding union, also comes and dwells in us.

Through the Eucharist, we can go forth knowing that our whole being has been permeated and invaded by the indwelling Trinity. The Spirit pours out God's love into our hearts (Rm 5:5) raising us to a new level of our unique goodness and beauty and dignity that God has effected through the Eucharist. St. Paul's words can aptly be applied to what happens in the Eucharist: "Your body, you know, is the temple of the Holy Spirit, who is in you since you received him from God" (1 Cor 6:19).

AN EMPTYING GOD

The Eucharist is the most powerful symbol of God's *kenotic* (from the Greek word: *kenosis*, an emptying; cf. Ph 2:7) love as we enter into Christ's self-emptying in His ever *now* renewing of His sacrifice on the cross for love of us. Christ's preaching, healing and above all His final hour on the cross all meet in the Eucharist as His sacrifice and sacrament, as the perfect imaging of the triune God's self-emptying for each of us.

Simone Weil once wrote: "If God had not been humiliated, in the person of Christ, he would be inferior to us." Nowhere else but in the Eucharist do we discover the perfect enactment of the paradox of God's perfection to consist in His desire to take His life and freely dispossess Himself of it in order that you and I and the whole human race might intimately share in His being.

> For God's foolishness is wiser than human wisdom,
> and God's weakness is stronger than human strength
> (1 Cor 1:25).

The God of Jesus manifests His perfection, not by being immutable and unchanging, but, rather, by His self-emptying out of love for us. The Eucharist brings us into the surrendering act of Jesus on the cross who leads us into the surrendering act of the Father, Son and Holy Spirit. God's power is His love, but it is a creative love of self-sacrifice unto suffering death. True power in God and in us is not to do innumerable acts of power over things. True and godly power is the creative love that allows God, Father, Son and Spirit, freely to empty Himself of His being in a total surrender in love for us.

In experiencing the triune God's sacrifice of Himself for love of us, we become divinized so as to share in His very own nature (2 P 1:4). If we share in God's divine nature which is self-emptying love unto death, then ought we not also to love one another through the power of the Eucharist?

INTIMACY WITH OTHERS

Love begets love and intimacy with others is the result of your sharing the intense intimacy of the Trinity. The reception of the Eucharist is not a mere receiving of an objective presence of Christ. Intimacy demands a response on your part to release the full power of the Spirit. Your sharing in God's intimate, ecstatic happiness breaks down all barriers and sends you forth to share your own being with others. You gain strength to give up your fears and aggressions and to begin to live in the power of God's self-sacrificing love.

It is in your receiving of the Eucharist that you attain a new oneness with the others in whom the same trinitarian life loves, especially within the context of the eucharistic celebration. Here is where the Church, the Body of Christ, comes together in loving union with its Head, Jesus Christ. The Liturgy is the sacred place and time when the Church is most realized by the power of the Holy Spirit. It is the realization of the life of the Church for which it exists: to praise and glorify God for the gifts of life and salvation we have received.

This intensification of the awareness of your belonging to *Church*, a greater consciousness of your being a living member of Christ's Body, brings to you also a greater awareness of Christ as the one who gives nourishment and sustenance to all other members in order that as a Body they can all live *in* Him. " . . . Christ who is the head by whom the whole body is fitted and joined together, every joint adding its own strength" (Ep 4:15-16). You become Christ and you become a new part of all of your brothers and sisters who are in Christ. St. Augustine uses strong language to illustrate this oneness in Christ:

> Let us rejoice and give thanks that we have become not only Christians but Christ. My brothers, do you understand the grace of God our Head? Stand in admiration, rejoice; we have become Christ.

As you and your fellow-worshippers receive the same Christ and enter into a new oneness with the Trinity, you are most powerfully united in a new sense of oneness with the uniqueness of each other. All of you symbolically enter into the depths of the richness of God's self-sacrificing love. You receive in the Eucharist the culmination of all the sacraments in which Christ encounters you and the other members of His Body in self-giving. Here is the greatest power of communication whereby Christ gives Himself to us in the complete gift of self-emptying on our behalf.

Likewise the fruit of the Eucharist is the begetting within you of the Spirit of love that empowers you to be sacrament and sacrifice of Christ toward all whom you meet. The full intensification of God's uncreated energies of love pours into you in the Eucharist. Abiding in Christ with the Father and the Holy Spirit, you are empowered to bring forth fruit in abundance. The fruit is a call to intimacy in a *comm-union*, a union with other human beings who with you are called in the Eucharist to become the Body of Christ.

> It is to the glory of my father that you should bear much fruit and then you will be my disciples . . . remain in my love. If you keep my commandments, you will remain in my love. This is my commandment: love one another as I have loved you (Jn 15:8-12).

LOVING A BROKEN WORLD

Not only do we join with Christ and the other members of His Body in the Eucharist to turn to the Father in His Spirit of love to surrender totally to do His holy will, but we together, Jesus the Head, and we, the conscious members of His Body, turn toward a broken world of suffering human beings. For do we truly receive Christ and the Father and the Holy Spirit in the Eucharist in their self-emptying love if we do not empty ourselves for others outside of the liturgical act of communion with God?

Have we really lifted our hearts to God in the Eucharist if we have not offered Him our whole being, with our whole set of relationships to other people who touch us and whom we touch in daily life? Of what avail is our offering of ourselves to God in the Church's liturgy if it is not completed in the offering of ourselves to our neighbors?

Again, Simone Weil dramatically puts it: "A victim of misfortune is lying in the road, half dead with hunger. God pities him but cannot send him bread. But I am here and luckily I am not God. I can give him a piece of bread. It is my one point of superiority over God."

TURNED TOWARD THE CROSS

Just as Jesus in the first eucharistic celebration with His disciples in the Last Supper was turned toward the sufferings and His death of the next day, so you and I turn toward creative suffering as we live in the eucharistic presence of Christ, and His Father and Spirit of love. Christ's eucharistic presence enlightens us to realize that true love is a self-emptying presence to all in need. Love is always a call to be available and vulnerable, just as Jesus in the Eucharist is a loving service toward us.

Openness in loving service toward others necessarily means the cross and suffering. If we wish to have a part with Christ, there is need of denying ourselves of all self-centeredness and to live in loving service for others. Our participation and sharing in the Body of Christ in the Eucharist are measured by the degree of sharing ourselves with each other before the Father of us all.

LOVING SERVICE

In the light of God's tremendous love for each of us individually, as especially experienced in the perfect, self-sacrificing of Jesus in the Eucharist for love of us, we can afford to move out of our fears and isolation in order to move toward others in loving service. We begin to see that we have a sense of inner dignity and beauty. God has given us many gifts that He wishes us to share in love through self-giving to others.

Living in the eucharistic presence of Christ means living our daily lives in His self-giving love to be available in love to others, no matter in what form of service that love may manifest itself. We are to go out and to be Eucharist to every man, woman and child that God sends into our lives. We are to "bear with one another charitably, in complete selflessness, gentleness and patience. Do all you can to preserve the unity of the Spirit by the peace that binds you together." (Ep 4:2-3).

Every talent and disposition God has put into you in your birth, through education and your life-experiences can now be developed in the love of the Spirit, a variety of gifts to build the same, one Body of Christ the Church (1 Cor 12:4). You are called to go forth from the Eucharist with the power of the risen Jesus within you to minister with Him to the needs of all you meet and are privileged to serve.

A COSMIC EUCHARIST

Now, as you live more and more consciously in the eucharistic presence of the triune community dwelling within you as *kenotic* or self-emptying divine persons for love of you, you move out into the created world. Now God's material creatures do not take you from His intimate, indwelling presence. That very presence allows you to find the same self-sacrificing love of God for His created universe in all of your relationships with creatures.

God is *now* creating His world. But He calls us, especially in the Eucharist, to the work of bringing unity of all things under Christ. "It was God who reconciled us to himself through Christ and gave us the work of handing on this reconciliation" (2 Cor 5:18). In humility we accept God's gift of our unique existence with all the hidden, undeveloped talents for creative work. We seek each day to use such gifts in loving service to build a better world.

As bread and wine in the Eucharist are not destroyed but by the Spirit of love are transformed into the self-emptying presence of Christ, so, too, all other material creatures are to be touched by us in creative love to transform into the cosmic Body of Christ. We no longer need to run from active involvement in the activities of our material world. Now, by living in the eucharistic presence of Jesus and emptying ourselves in our works and sufferings out of love for Christ, neighbor and all of His creation, we extend the presence of Jesus into the cosmos.

Whatever we do in unselfish love to make this a better world to live in, be it to bake a pie, protest abortion, fight bigotry and racism, we are not only living in the presence of the eucharistic Lord but we are sharing in His priesthood as victim and offerer to bring about the cosmic Eucharist. By living and acting in the presence of Jesus in the Eucharist we are con-

tributing to the fulfillment of God's initial plan actualized only
by the self-sacrifice and self-present sacrament of Christ to the
world.

Then St. Paul's vision will become a reality through our
loving cooperation:

> There is only Christ.
> He is everything,
> and he is in everything (Col 3:11).

Chapter Seven

Trinitarian Indwelling Presence

We were all made for love, to be loved and to love. But no word has been so abused and misunderstood as to its true meaning as the word, *love*. The *Playboy* understanding of love is centered on man, the egoist in search of human "objects" to satisfy his sense pleasures. Such love does not go out to discover one's uniqueness in unselfish giving to another but it turns in a sickly way toward itself.

So often we Christians in our loving relations toward God and other human persons may also conceive love as receiving from and not a self-emptying toward another. In prayer and in the sacraments we wish to receive from God consolations, good feelings, security from eternal death; above all we desire *graces* to make our lives on earth pleasant and to guarantee for all eternity a pleasant existence.

Recently George Gallup Jr. interviewed 1,000 Roman Catholics and asked them what they sought from their religion. The majority replied that they hoped to obtain *health*, *happiness* and *Heaven*.

Love, when it is true, is self-emptying. It is a movement toward another whom we wish to serve and bring into our complete happiness. It is not so much that we are ready to die for the other. It is more that we wish that the other live immortally, forever, that the divine in that person come forth and burst into ultimate, unending happiness.

GOD IS LOVE THAT IS INTIMATE

God is love by His very own nature. Giving and sharing is not only His name, but this is His nature. He created this universe and brought forth creatures all in order to extend Himself and share Himself with the chef d'oeuvre of all of His creation: man and woman. God creates non-human beings and gives them to human persons only that in and through these gifts we human beings might reach a communion with God and share intimately in the gift of God Himself to us.

In the Book of *Genesis* we read of two different accounts of the creation of the first man and woman. In Gn 1:26, *man* is a generic term, standing for both man and woman. God has made man according to His own image and likeness. Nothing is hinted at as to the origin of man or how his body was formed. Man is found in a world teeming with plants, birds, fish and animals and commanded to fill the earth and subdue it. There is no distinction between man and woman. Both are included in the commission to go forth in creative work to dominate the world around them and from which they differ by reason of being made according to the image and likeness of a God who is powerful and creative.

In the second account of Adam and Eve (Gn 2:7, 15, 18, 21-23), however, we see Adam first created out of the earth. He is a part of the material world and lives in the Garden of Eden. God gives him a charge, not to subdue and dominate, control and possess, but to tend and care the garden. He takes care of the material world around him with love and concern. But God sees that Adam is lonely. God decides to create for him a companion, one who can share intimately with Adam a life, ideas, ideals, concerns, but, above all, in intimate love to share herself in self-giving and to bring forth new human life in that love. God is reflected now to them, not as a doing God, but as an intimate, self-giving God who is experienced in the intimacy of human love of two persons for each other. "No one has ever seen God; but as long as we love one another, God will live in us and his love will be complete in us" (1 Jn 4:12).

Our call to live in intimacy with each other comes out of God's very own nature as a community in loving, self-giving relationships to each member of the triune community to which love brings about a oneness in nature and distinction in person. The mystery of the Trinity has been revealed to us in Holy Scripture. Especially this was the work of the Word that became flesh and dwelt among us that we might know the Father through seeing Him in His Son (Jn 14:9) and we would recognize them as unique persons in the same Spirit of love.

THE OUTPOURING OF THE TRINITY

God's fullest revelation is made in His incarnate Word, Jesus Christ. For in Him we have not only words, but we have the one Word that is the perfect copy of God's nature, but in human form. In Him we can come, not only to know God's very nature as love and self-giving, but through His outpoured Spirit we can be brought into a loving communion with God's very own being. We can become truly participators of God's very own nature (2 P 1:4).

The author of the *Letter to the Hebrews* describes this revelation through God's incarnate Word:

> . . . but in our own time, the last days, he has spoken to us through his Son, the Son that he has appointed to inherit everything and through whom he made everything there is. He is the radiant light of God's glory and the perfect copy of his nature, sustaining the universe by his powerful command; and now that he has destroyed the defilement of sin, he has gone to take his place in heaven at the right hand of divine Majesty. So he is now as far above the angels as the title which he has inherited is higher than their own name (Heb 1:2-4).

By knowing the Word incarnate, we can now know the Father and His Spirit in whom the Word makes known to us the Father. The very self-giving of the Father of Himself to the Son through the Spirit of love and the returned self-giving of the Son to the Father in the same intimate Spirit of love became the basis of the Good News that God wishes to catch us up into that same family intimacy of the Trinity. Jesus Christ, through His Spirit, bridges the abyss of our inability ever to come to know and experience God as He is in truth and love. Now it is possible to experience God's nature as a community of self-giving persons through Jesus Christ. "Everything has been entrusted to me by my Father; and no one knows the Son except the Father, just as no one knows the Father except the Son and those to whom the Son chooses to reveal him" (Mt 11:27).

A MYSTERY TO BE EXPERIENCED

How sad that for the majority of Christians the great mystery of the Trinity at the heart of all reality, at the beginning of all creation emptying itself of its life in order that creatures may participate in that life and at the end of all creation that we are to experience this intimate self-giving of a Father, Son and Spirit, is only a dogma to which they give a mere intellectual assent. Karl Rahner laments this fact that most Christians remain "monotheists," that is, they pray to a God who is outside or up there but they fail to experience God as a community of loving and self-giving persons living intimately within the Christians. He writes:

> . . . despite their orthodox confession of the Trinity, Christians are, in their practical life, almost mere "monotheists." We must be willing to admit that, should the doctrine of the Trinity have to be dropped as false, the major part of religious literature

could well remain virtually unchanged . . . (K. Rahner: *The Trinity*: pp. 10-11).

But how can we experience God, Father, Son and Holy Spirit, whom Scripture says no human being has ever been able to see and still live? We surely can never know God perfectly as He is in His essence or we would have to be essentially of the same nature as God. We can never see Him fully. "No one has ever seen God" (1 Jn 4:12). In spite of God's revelation about His nature and His activities as revealed through Jesus Christ, we shall never know Him fully.

Yet the good news is that this all-loving God is not far from us. In Him, the unknown God, we live and move and have our being (Ac 17:28). Although there will always remain something unapproachable, unpossessable and unfathomable about God, the Trinity, yet Jesus Christ's role in His incarnation, death, resurrection is to pour the love of God into our hearts (Rm 5:5) through the Spirit that is given to us so that we can "know" and experience God as a community of loving persons.

This Trinity abides in us at all times. God touches us in His uncreated energies of love. The unique, personalistic relations of Father, Son and Holy Spirit burst forth from the Trinity and continue to touch us and swirl around us at all times in the context of the present moment. There can be no place or time in which the uncreated energies of God's love do not bombard, invade, penetrate us at all times. All this tremendous love, calling us into intimate sharing of God's very own being, is going on within us and around us at all times. We go to prayer now, not any longer to change God's attitude toward us, but rather to receive the Trinity's outpoured love in the self-giving of each person to us individually so that we can be changed by the *I-Thou* in the *We* community of the Trinity into His loving children. We live now in "mystery" through an increase of faith, hope and love that God, Father, Son and Spirit, are to be found inside of each event as uncreated energies of love.

All you have to do is simply allow yourself to be carried along in each hour, surrendering to the "insideness" of God's energies of love. You cooperate with God in all things, little or big. Live this present moment in that inner awareness that you are never alone but that you flow out of God's tremendous personalized love that calls you into your true, authentic *I-ness*. Such an awareness of belonging to the very family of God removes from you all fear. You give up any aggressiveness to attack anyone who might threaten you in your false security of the person you have felt yourself to be through your own power and not the power of God's weakness that loves you into your true being.

GOD WITHIN YOU

Brother Lawrence, the 17th century Carmelite brother, who practiced so faithfully the presence of the indwelling Trinity as he went about his simple chores of cooking in the monastery kitchen, writes:

> Since knowledge is a measurement of love, the deeper and more intimate you are with Him, the greater will be your love for Him. And if our love for the Lord is great, then we will love Him as much during grief as in joy. . . . So seek him often by faith. Oh, dear friend, the Lord is not outside of you, pouring down favors. The Lord is within you. Seek Him there, within . . . and nowhere else. . . . Dear friend, would you now begin, today, to be devoted to the Lord, in earnest? Cast everything else out of your heart. He would possess it alone. Beg of Him that favor (Letter 16).

This reality was the end of the incarnation, death and resurrection of Jesus Christ. He came among us to make it possible, not only that we might become children of God, but that at all times we might live in that continued awareness discovered in each moment of our lives. This is your human dignity: to be called children of God; and you really are such in the process of discovering and surrendering to the uncreated energies of God living within you and within the context of each human situation or event. God is saying in substance to you: "Here I am; this place is holy. Take off your shoes, your securities, and approach this burning bush to become consumed by the fire of My divine love for you."

This highest union, the infused union of the Trinity, in which God communicates Himself as Father, Son and Spirit, is not achieved by any conceptual knowledge but through an immediate, experiential knowledge wherein He opens Himself to you. You can never come to this knowledge through your own concepts or thinking process. God, purely and simply in His transcendence, reveals Himself to you when He wishes. It is not so much that God does something new and different to you after years of your own preparation and cooperation through continued purification of your heart from self-centeredness. He is always present, the same loving Father, Son and Spirit, loving you with an infinite, uncreated love.

But when you have cracked open the doors of your heart and you finally open them, you stand before what was always there. "Behold I stand at the door and I knock. He who opens, I will enter and sup with him" (Rv 3:20). In a state of humility, you break yourself of your own power to possess your life to take love and to control both God and others. Then you enter into the reality that always was there. With Moses we have to climb up the mountain to reach God by a knowing that is an unknowing, a darkness that is truly luminous. As you separate yourself from all limitations you place on God and from all attachments to your own self-love, you reach the top of the mountain. There in the darkness of the storming clouds you

hear the notes of the trumpet and you see those lights that no
human method could ever give you. No human mind, no
guru, no technique could ever bring you God's personalized
gift of Himself. God has to take over and communicate Himself directly. No one but God can give Himself to you. It is
sheer gift, but the gift is God Himself.

This is the awesome mystery of the good news: that we can
experience God sharing with us His very own being and divinizing us into His own children.

> Think of the love that the Father has lavished on us,
> by letting us be called God's children;
> and that is what we are. . . .
> My dear people, we are already the children of God
> but what we are to be in the future has not yet been revealed;
> all we know is, that when it is revealed
> we shall be like him
> because we shall see him as he really is (1 Jn 3:1-2).

LIVING IN GOD'S PRESENCE

Your goal in life is to convert your life at every moment
into love. You want to move your will so that at each moment
you wish to surrender yourself in total gift back to God. This
can only be done to the degree that you experience in each
moment God's great love for you. God is completely and totally
present to you in His self-giving. God, Father, Son and Holy
Spirit cannot be more present or more self-giving than He is to
you at this moment in this present situation. The question is:
how can you become more present to Him?

To give, not things, but ultimately of oneself, is the essence of love. Love lavishes goods, gives all without reserve if
the love that you receive is consciously experienced from God
as a similar love without reserve. Love begets the same kind of
love experienced. How can you continue ever more to experi-

ence this infinite love? How can you hold yourself in the state of oneness, your will attached solely at all times to the will of God? This is God's gift through His Spirit. It comes through infused faith, hope and love. Yet you can cooperate to dispose yourself for this increased gift of awareness of God's intimate, loving presence in each moment. No one but yourself can raise your mind and heart toward God and gift God with the free gift of yourself. But this gifting of yourself to God takes place in the context of your every moment, in the deeds, words and thoughts that you permeate with your self-giving love to God.

You can change your life gradually by pushing yourself gently under the movement of the Spirit of love to align yourself in all your being with the being of God as self-giving love. You wish to do all to please God. You desire to have no desire but to glorify God. He becomes your magnificent obsession. Every thought, word and deed becomes motivated by the desire to love God with your whole heart. This is the primary command, the great dignity to which you have been called when God created you "according to the image and likeness" of Christ, His only begotten Son. By striving to become what you are in God's love you reach the state of inner harmony that is manifested by peace and joy. Only then can you become love toward others, a presence of self-gifting to all whom you meet. The true test of how intimately you live in the presence of the Trinity is how intensely you strive to live intimately with each person who comes into your life.

Chapter Eight

Light From Light

In the Christian East mystics speak about the Taboric Light that shines within all Christians. This very scriptural symbol becomes an archetypal symbol of the presence of the risen Jesus Christ living within the Christian who dies to self and surrenders to the indwelling presence of Christ. What many of the ancient mystics of the East experienced was a progressive awareness of themselves becoming one with Christ. As they surrendered to His divinizing Spirit, they entered into an experience that became constant and ever growing that they called "seeing the Taboric Light" within them.

On Tabor, Jesus was transfigured in glory. ". . . we had seen his majesty for ourselves. He was honored and glorified by God the Father, when the Sublime Glory itself spoke to him and said, 'This is my Son, the Beloved; he enjoys my favor.' We heard this ourselves, spoken from heaven when we were with him on the holy mountain" (2 P 1:17-18). "There in their presence he was transfigured: his face shone like the sun and his clothes became as white as the light" (Mt 17:2).

Such Eastern Fathers saw themselves as sharers in the light of the transfigured Christ. St. Symeon the New Theologian (†1022) is representative of such Eastern Christian mystics in his description of the indwelling Christ as light within the Christian:

O stupendous prodigy, of an incomprehensible God, who works and yet is mysteriously incomprehensible! A man bears consciously in himself God as light, Him who has produced and created all things, holding even the man who carries Him. Man carries Him interiorly as a treasure which transcends words, written or spoken, any quality, quantity, image, matter and figure, shaped in an inexplicable beauty, all entirely simply as *light*, He who transcends all light.

CHRIST, THE LIGHT OF THE WORLD

Does not Holy Scripture describe God in the fullness of His perfections as light? "God is light; there is no darkness in him at all" (1 Jn 1:5). When God's Word came into our broken world, the Gospel of St. John describes Him as both the fullness of all shared life in this world and as the light that battles darkness:

> All that came to be had life in him
> and that life was the light of men,
> a light that shines in the dark,
> a light that darkness could not overpower. . . .
> The Word was the true light
> that enlightens all men (Jn 1:4,5,9).

Jesus often refers to Himself as light: "I, the light, have come into the world so that whoever believes in me need not stay in the dark any more" (Jn 12:46). When He preached in the synagogue at Nazareth at the beginning of His public ministry, He quoted from Isaiah 61: "He has sent me to bring the good news to the poor, to proclaim liberty to captives and to the blind new sight, to set the downtrodden free . . . " (Lk 4:18). He entered into the darkness within the daily lives of those whom He met on this earth and led them into the light of His healing love.

Our Christian faith tells us that by our Baptism, we are

inserted into the risen Christ. He is still a light that drives out the darkness from within us. He is a living light, a consciousness-center of love living inside of us where He abides with His Father and the Spirit of love. He promised that if we were His disciples and were to keep His commands, He and the Father would come and abide in us (Jn 14:23). We are already by our Baptism a holy temple of God, in whom dwells the Holy Spirit (1 Cor 3:16, 6:19).

CHRIST DWELLING WITHIN US

By the mystery of the resurrection Jesus Christ inhabits us from within. This sublime mystery is described by a 13th century monk:

> In me, in my most interior Jesus is present. All outside of our heart is only to discover the treasure hidden interiorly in the heart. There is found that sepulcher of Easter and there the new life. "Woman, why do you weep? Whom do you seek? Whom you seek, you already possess and you do not know Him? You have the true, eternal joy and still you weep? It is more intimate to your being and still you seek it outside! You are there, outside, weeping near the tomb. Your heart is my tomb. And I am not there dead, but I repose there, living always. Your soul is My garden. You are right when you believed that I was the gardener. I am the New Adam. I work and supervise My paradise. Your tears, your love, your desire, all this is My work. You possess Me at the most intimate level of your being, without knowing it and this is why you seek Me outside. It is then outside also that I appeared to you and also that I make you to return to yourself, to make you find at the intimacy of your being Him whom you seek outside."

Our growth in perfection consists in the intensity of union that we attain through the conscious awareness we have of Jesus Christ living and operating within us as we surrender

totally ourselves to His inner guidance. We strive to live in a
perfect *symbiosis*, a life with Him of two wills operating as one
through the union brought about by the Holy Spirit.

This living Christ is given to you in the fullness of His
resurrectional life. Yet in a way He is born into your consciousness as an embryo that is to grow as you yield to His real
presence, as you cooperate with Him by putting every thought
and act under His guiding light. St. Paul considered his role as
a midwife to bring forth the life of Christ in the hearts of his
Christians. And this life, he considered, developed as the individual Christian surrendered to the lordship of Christ risen.
". . . every thought is our prisoner, captured to be brought
into obedience to Christ. Once you have given your complete
obedience, we are prepared to punish any disobedience"
(2 Cor 10:5-6).

THE LIGHT SHINES IN DARKNESS

Jesus Christ is present within you as a light that powerfully
dissipates the darkness that is also indwelling within you. What
clouds of darkness of selfishness cover you from within you
and impede you from letting the light of Christ transform you
into light! What fears are locked deeply within you! And such
fears spawn other forms of fear as doubts, anxieties, dread,
worries, hatred, anger, horror, fright or terror of the past, the
present and the future.

Deep down within you is Christ. And your true self is there
waiting to be born into His life. The Spirit of the risen Jesus
hovers over this inner chaos and darkness that resist that
birthing of yourself into Christ. Your true self cannot be
brought to birth by yourself. Your identity as an *I* can only be
discovered in the *Thou* of Jesus Christ in whom you find your
reason for being. He alone is the Divine Physician who posses-

ses the fullness of life in Himself because He is the true image of the invisible God.

It is only through the Holy Spirit released by the indwelling, risen Jesus that we can know the full Jesus Christ and our true selves in loving oneness with Him. "We know that he lives in us by the Spirit that he has given us" (1 Jn 3:24). This Spirit of love fills us with faith in God's great love in Christ Jesus and faith in that living and loving Christ abiding intimately within us. We are filled with hope by that Spirit that the risen Lord has conquered sin and death and we can meet this indwelling, risen Lord in all of our darkness and inauthenticity. The Spirit fills us with the hopeful realization that our fully integrated persons, the ones that we should be by God's unique love for each of us, can be realized only by the interacting, loving relationships of the Father, Son and Holy Spirit.

A GREATER THAN I

Gabriel Marcel, the French philosopher, writes about this existential hope given to us by the Spirit of Jesus risen: "I can be led to recognize that deep down in me there is something other than me, something further within me than I am myself." Inside of you, beyond the swirling of the outside of the cyclone or tornado, is the eye or core that brings together a centering of peace and power, healing love and strength. That center is the indwelling Christ that we can touch intimately through faith, hope and love and be touched. He is the Center of the world and resides at your center. He is the *Alpha* and the *Omega*, "who is, who was, and who is to come, the Almighty" (Rv 1:8). Jesus risen stands as light shining in our brokenness and whispers from the depths of our being:

Do not be afraid; it is I, the First and the Last; I am the Living

One, I was dead and now I am to live for ever and ever, and I hold the keys of death and of the underworld. (Rv 1:17-18).

If this divine Center is at the core of your being, how is it you are not aware of this basic truth, this "good news"? The transfigured Christ, gloriously risen, who has conquered all sin and death is within you and more powerful than anything or anyone outside of you (1 Jn 4:4). It is you, like the three Apostles, Peter, James and John, who do not quite see Him in all His transfiguring light at all times. "There in their presence he was transfigured" (Mk 9:2).

METANOIA

You are called to die to the darkness of self-centeredness in your life, so that in a conversion you may perceive what has always been within you from the time of your Baptism, the light of Christ ready to transfigure you into His same glorious light. Jesus Christ in His earthly preaching demanded repentance of His followers. This was a turnabout in one's total attitude and in the use of one's powers. Positively it was a turning totally toward God. But this turning toward God's presence as transfiguring love can be accomplished only if one is ready to turn away from selfishness (sinning) and is ready to live by a new orientation toward God as one's true center. Such a new life is given by the Holy Spirit but only on condition that we not only *affectively* but also *effectively* seek this new life, a new sharing in Christ by doing all we can to move toward God as Center of our lives.

The first step toward a new orientation from darkness to live in the light of Christ dwelling within you is to be firmly persuaded by God's revealed words in Scripture and the teaching of the Church that Jesus Christ truly lives in all His transcendent light and power within you. He has already taken the initiative. It is for you to respond to this reality of the indwelling Christ as light within you. Joy, thanksgiving, adoration, but above all, worship and complete surrender of yourself to Christ and His Father in the Spirit of love that inundates you continually with this interior knowledge of God's presence as intimate love abiding within you are part of your response.

The second step toward living in the presence of Christ as light within you is to strive to increase the faith, hope and love that have been infused into you in your Baptism. Rooted in God's revelation concerning His transcendence, His nature as love and self-giving and through the risen Lord Jesus His immanence as indwelling within you, you can turn inwardly to a different level than the habitual, busy, doing level of your ordinary consciousness that allows you to concentrate on your creative work in a material world. This other level can co-exist as another level of consciousness that can become stronger and stronger as God's infusion of faith, hope and love becomes stronger. Such an infusion creates within you a new knowledge that surpasses all human understanding.

By recalling often the indwelling presence of Christ as light within you and surrendering to His inner guidance as you seek in love to be obedient to Him, you can cultivate higher levels of this inner consciousness. What is important in such acts of recalling the presence of the indwelling Christ is not our conscious experience of this inner reality. What is important is the reality of Jesus Christ of whom we become aware and to whom we surrender ourselves. Such conscious experience is the medium through which alone God can be found. Thus the psychological repercussions are not important. Yet only if we have a personal awareness of Christ indwelling us can He become present to us in a way that we can surrender to a real person.

LIVING IN THE LIGHT OF CHRIST

Is it possible for you and me and all other human beings immersed in the material world of so much motion, activity and multiplicity that requires concentration on the work at hand to be also centered upon the indwelling presence of Christ? Can a teacher, a preacher, a farmer, a housewife, a student, a taxi-driver, an accountant, an athlete live on two levels at the same time? Can you personally be yourself completely on the "outside" level of your ordinary living in contact with material beings outside of you and still maintain an "inward" attentiveness to the Divine Guest that dwells within you?

St. Paul challenged the Thessalonians, ordinary converts to Christianity from all walks of life, to "pray constantly": "Be happy at all times; pray constantly; and for all things give thanks to God, because this is what God expects you to do in Christ Jesus" (1 Th 5:17-18). To pray always was considered as a state of awareness that could be reached by the working of the Holy Spirit in the depths of the heart of the individual Christian as he or she stood vigilant and called out for that presence of God to be realized through the medium of human consciousness.

For that reason the early Christians who fled into the desert in a continued state of conversion strove to become present to the indwelling Christ by calling upon His name and entering into the presence of the risen Lord. Although the culture and many other aspects of our modern 20th century living differ vastly from the culture of those Christians living in the early centuries of Christianity, yet the Christian of the Bronx and the Christian of the Egyptian desert of the 4th century are called upon to be attentive to the presence of the indwelling Lord and to surrender their entire life to His guidance, in obedience to His will out of love for Him who loves us infinitely.

MOVING TOWARD CENTER

The secret of living the true Christian life under the guidance of the inner light of Christ indwelling at center lies in a continuously renewed immediacy of Christ's presence and loving activity. If you wish to be consciously aware of Christ's indwelling presence as light and yield to His guidance, you are called to a continued turning inward to become centered upon your Center. This means the mental discipline of moving your will by your own desire, for no one, not even God, can do this desiring for you. It is to be your consciousness as the medium by which you come into the already present light of Christ.

A beautiful, modern Christian, Dr. Frank C. Laubach (†1970) spent many years in missionary work as a Congregationalist missionary on the island of Mindanao in the southern Philippines helping a fierce tribe, the Maranaws, a Muslim people famous for their anti-Christian attitudes, to become literate by developing for them a written language in which they could read about the good news of Jesus Christ. Alone before his wife and child joined him, he spent his solitude in developing the presence of the indwelling Christ that he had discovered in the writings of Brother Lawrence, the 17th century Carmelite cook.

Laubach writes about his own attempts to remain more and more consciously present to the indwelling Lord:

> Can we have that contact with God all the time?
> All the time awake, fall asleep in His arms,
> and awaken in His presence.
> Can we attain that? Can we do His will all the time? Can
> we think His thoughts all the time? . . .
> We do not think of one thing. We always think of the relationship of at least two things, and more often of three or more things simultaneously. So my problem is this: Can I bring God

back in my mind-flow every few seconds so that God shall always be in my mind as an afterimage, shall always be one of the elements in every concept and percept?
I choose to make the rest of my life an experiment in answering this question.

Patiently and with great inner discipline, he worked for years. When he discovered that he had turned away from his Center, he humbled himself and courageously started in again. He discovered that it did no good to strain, but in free abandonment and trusting in God's gift of faith and His indwelling presence, he pushed each day to discover God in the beauties of nature around him, in the natives whom he chose to serve as Christ Himself, but also within the inner sanctuary of his heart. He discovered that it was impossible to maintain that concentration all the time but he strove first to do it every hour on the hour. Then he sought to turn within each half hour. He found that he had gradually, over weeks, months and years formed a habit that made it easy to live in the presence of God. God had become *real* to him and it became natural for him to live *with* Christ and to be *in* Him.

Is such a practice possible for you? Only if you are called in a conversion to want to become more present to God intimately present to you, and you are willing to move away from dispersion of your attention to become habitually centered on God. The light of Christ is there within you. Like a leaven, He permeates from within every part of your body and mind and spirit. Each moment is given to you so that you may surrender yourself to His inner light and be transformed also into a sharing even now of His glorious resurrection.

His light within you is not a physical light that you should strive to see. It is an inner, transcendent light that has no form. Yet it is something that can be experienced as "localized" in your "heart," in the deepest levels of your consciousness as a new knowledge and presence that you can by God's grace and your cooperation habitually be aware of in ever-increasing degrees. This continued state of living in the light of Christ and surrendering to His lordship is the gift of contemplation.

A LIGHT TO THE WORLD

As you yield to Christ's transforming light from within you, the same Spirit of the risen Lord urges you to let the transforming light of Jesus pour through your transfigured oneness with Him to become His light and presence of love to the world around you. This admits of an infinity of growth. "I am the light of the world; anyone who follows me will not be walking in the dark; he will have the light of life" (Jn 8:12). Your heart is becoming enlightened and your whole being is made lightsome (Mt 6:22).

The inner light of Christ leading you into the light of the indwelling Trinity suffuses your entire being as you joyfully experience in every thought, word and deed the exhilarating joy of being a child of God. God has called you "out of darkness into his wonderful light" (1 P 2:9).

But the light of Christ is to shine through you outward toward others.

> You are the light of the world. A city built on a hill-top cannot be hidden. No one lights a lamp to put it under a tub; they put it on the lampstand where it shines for everyone in the house. In the same way your light must shine in the sight of men, so that, seeing your good works, they may give the praise to your Father in heaven (Mt 5:14-16).

Jesus is risen and lives within you as light and raises you from your darkness into a sharing of His risen life. But His Spirit of love drives you out to become Christ's translucent light of new life and love to all you meet. You now have the power, to the degree that you have become light from Christ's light, to bring the same transfiguring light to the world that lies in darkness of brokenness and self-centeredness all around you. Christ can become light for them only if you and like-minded Christians allow His light of love to go through you into the darkness of others. You breathe the name of Jesus and His light-presence over each person you meet and you believe, as you have experienced within yourself, that they also can rise to a sharing in His risen glory and become less dark and more of loving light in the world.

Let me close this chapter by quoting parts of a poem I wrote called: *Firefly*:

> Why is there light
>   and then the silent darkness
>   soon broken by soft light?
> Why not total light
>   all the time
>   dispelling all the night's darkness?
>
> O Christ, be the light,
> *Phos Hilaron*, Radiant Light,
>   that I may carry
>   into the world's darkness.
> Make me a carrier of Your light,
>   that I may be
>   flashing light across the night.
>
> In the night I stretch out
>   to embrace Your light.
> Come, Bright Light of love,
>   phosphorize my being!
> May Your light be total,
>   not on or off,
>   but may it consume
>   the darkness in me.
>
> O Christ, be full noon to me!

Or if night must be,
may Your light be constant,
   not flashing, off and on.
May I carry Your light,
   be Your light to others,
      who sleep in the dark of night.

Chapter Nine

Listening to the Inner Word

In the powerful story of courage shown by Helen Keller in the play about her growth into humanity by means of communication in love given her by her patient teacher, Annie Sullivan, there is a climax scene that heralds a breakthrough. The teacher over and over with immense patience had signed the simple word, *water*, in the hand of the child, Helen. But one day she signed it and placed Helen's hand under the pump's spout. As the water flowed over her hand, a new world named *water* and *Helen* was born as the communicating word from out of God's mind leapt from the child's hand to her mind and then out to a new world of reality, God's reality.

St. Augustine defined man as one who is *capax Dei*, capable of knowing and loving God. But we have been made for this potentiality only because we are also *capax mundi*, capable of receiving God's communication in knowledge and love in and through the world around us.

GOD'S WORD IN CREATION

If God's essence is love, as Judaeo-Christianity reveals to us, then He is always seeking to share His being by communicating His presence to us, whom He created according to His image and likeness (Gn 1:26) through His Word. God becomes a God-toward-others by communicating Himself in the gifts of creation through His Word and His Spirit of love. The entire world around us is being created in a process of God's sign of His burning desire to give Himself in faithful communication to us through His Word. The world at its interior is filled with the self-communicating Trinity. God is filling the universe with His loving Self. His uncreated energies swirl through and fill all creatures with His loving, creative presence. ". . . Yahweh's love fills the earth. By the word of Yahweh the heavens were made, their whole array by the breath of his mouth" (Ps 33:5-6).

Everything flows out of God's exuberant fullness of being and *becomes* a reality in His communicating Word. God is present in the heavens and on the earth. "Can anyone hide in a dark corner without my seeing him?—it is Yahweh who speaks. Do I not fill heaven and earth?—it is Yahweh who speaks" (Jr 23:24). And this loving, communicating God speaks to us constantly through His word in the oceans and mountains, birds and beasts, flowers and all living things that spring into being under His laughing, joyful gaze. Nothing that is can escape His loving touch, His presence as Giver of life.

Not only does God communicate Himself in creation, but he is a sustaining, directing God. He evolves His presence that is locked into His creation through His Word that is continually being communicated over millions of years. No human being can complain that God has never spoken His word to him or her. St. Paul clearly shows the universality to all human beings of God's revelation of Himself in all creation:

> For what can be known about God is perfectly plain to them since God himself has made it plain. Ever since God created the world his everlasting power and deity—however invisible— have been there for the mind to see in the things he has made. That is why such people are without excuse: they knew God and yet refused to honor him as God or to thank him; instead,

they made nonsense out of logic and their empty minds were darkened. (Rm 1:19-21).

GOD'S LOGOS IN MAN

Of all the millions of creatures made by God, man and woman alone remain unfinished and open-ended. God speaks to them in the coolness of evening in the Garden of Eden. Our human uniqueness consists in being made in the image of God. Through possessing an intellect and will, we are able to enter into communication and ultimately communion with God to share His very own happiness and nature as being love. We can posit ourselves as an *I*, dependent on the Absolute *I* of God. We are being summoned by God continually in every moment of our existence, in each event, to receive God's Word actively. We are called to be listeners of God's Word, to understand and to believe in His Word.

We are not propelled into our uniqueness as individuals by a pre-determined guidance on God's part. His only determination is to invite and call us to accept our existence by means of a decision to live according to God's Word.

RESTING IN GOD'S WORD

God calls us to receive His love through the communication of His Word in His Spirit of love. But the language of love is silence. If we are to listen to God's Word, we are in need of silencing the noisiness within our hearts and around us in the multiplied world that is orientated in its brokenness toward "sin and death," symbols of self-centeredness and a movement away from God-centeredness. The condition that served as criterion of one's docility in listening to the Word of God was measured by the early Christians who inhabited the deserts in terms of resting in the Lord or quieting all inordinate desires. Teilhard de Chardin calls such a listening state "passionate indifference," whereby Christians surrender themselves totally to God dwelling and revealing Himself within the living temple of God that Christians are.

This state of listening is comparable to the seventh day of rest that the Lord took after His labors of creating the world. It is the new day of rest, the day of *kairos* time of salvation in which we human beings opt always to do that which most pleases the Heavenly Father according to His Word. This is described in the *Letter to the Hebrews*:

> . . . the promise of reaching the place of rest he had for them still holds good, and none of you must think that he has come too late for it. We received the Good News exactly as they did; but hearing the message did them no good because they did not share the faith of those who listened . . . There must still be, therefore, a place of rest reserved for God's people, the seventh-day rest, since to reach the place of rest is to rest after your work as God did after His. We must therefore do everything we can to reach this place of rest, or some of you might copy this example of disobedience and be lost (Heb 4:1-11).

Jesus speaks of the necessity of our entering into our "inner closet" when we wish to pray, and there we are to pray in spirit and in truth to the Heavenly Father (Mt 6:6). Scripture and the early Christian writers referred to this innermost self as our "heart." It is into our heart, into the deepest reaches of our consciousness, that we enter in order to come face to face in silence with God. In utter openness and receptivity we wait without any preconceived ideas of what Jesus, the Word of the Father, will reveal to us from within us and from without, in the world events around us of this new day.

Jesus Christ, the mighty Word that goes forth from the mouth of Yahweh and returns fulfilled (Is 55:11-12), is so utterly ineffable, so beyond any conceptualization that, as soon as you think you have understood His message, in that moment you have introduced noise.

A DESERT EMPTYING

The moment you settle down like the Israelites with the flesh pots of Egypt and assent that now you know Jesus Christ, then you have lost Him. God's Word is a living Word, a two-edged sword.

> The word of God is something alive and active: it cuts like any double-edged sword but more finely: it can slip through the place where the soul is divided from the spirit, or joints from the marrow; it can judge the secret emotions and thoughts. No created thing can hide from him; everything is uncovered and open to the eyes of the one to whom we must give account of ourselves (Heb 4:12-13).

God's Word is so overwhelmingly great and alive that no human being can know Him completely or control Him in His Word that He is constantly speaking at each moment. We know God's Word by not knowing Him, by not limiting God's power to reveal and communicate Himself to us in any way He wishes. He is love infinite and no one can love Him enough to say that now he or she can stop growing in love. But knowing and loving God means first to listen to His revealing Word and then in the desert experience of meeting the awesome God in His Word to surrender to God in intimate communion. This necessitates in our listening a *kenosis*, an emptying, in order that God may fill the void.

Thomas Merton describes this experience as a higher kind of listening, not a mere receptivity to a certain kind of message, but a general emptying "that waits to realize the fullness of the message of God within its own apparent void. The true con-

templative . . . remains empty because he knows that he can
never expect or anticipate the word that will transform his
darkness into light" (*Contemplative Prayer*: p. 112).

GOD'S EXTERIOR COMMUNICATION

A general emptying of our own driving, aggressive attacks
upon God, others and the world around us and a putting on of
a gentle spirit to listen to God as He communicates Himself to
us is necessary if we are to be in touch with God as He communicates Himself to us both from outside and from
within ourselves.

God reveals Himself through His Word as found in Holy
Scripture. This requires a listening on the levels of body, soul
and spirit as God's message comes to us as history, an intellectual message to us. Then God's Spirit speaks not only a
special healing word of love in the broken time and space in
which we listen to this word but He also releases the dynamic
power of God that gives faith and hope in God's will to fulfill
what His Spirit of love reveals.

We approach listening to the Word of God in Scripture
with humility and gratitude, but above all with child-like faith
that God's Word made flesh is still with us unto the end of the
world in His revealed Word (Mt 28:20); yet it is always a fresh,
new Word being given to us as we listen with complete inner
attentiveness and in deep faith, hope and love. Such listening
to Scripture is not merely a dry study, an intellectual exercise,
but it is a heart-to-heart encounter with Jesus Christ, the same
yesterday, today and always (Heb 13:8). This living Word
speaks to us of the Father's infinite, tender love for us individually and for the entire human race, called to form the Body of
Christ. That same Word, Jesus Christ, in all His glorious resurrectional presence within us, pours out His Spirit so that we
can truly have new ears to receive the seed of God's Word.

Such listening means that we also are listening to God in His revelation within the Church in its authority to teach and preach God's Word from Scripture and from the living traditions developed continually as the hierarchical members teach with their special charism the other members of the Church.

LISTENING TO GOD IN OTHER PERSONS

A special listening to God's Word as an unfolding of God's loving presence is developed as you learn to listen to God in others. Here you can see from your own experience what inner attentiveness and love are required if you are truly to listen to God in the presence of other persons who meet you and communicate themselves to you through their words and their being. At first we listen on the bodily level to God's Word speaking to us through others. We seek to praise God in the positive qualities found in those we encounter. Everyone has some negative qualities but we seek in each encounter to move from the bodily level into a faith, hope and love vision that will allow us to pierce beyond the evident negative side of the person to see deeper the Word of God and to listen to what message of beauty and love the Word is speaking from within that person.

This will require on your part a respect for the uniqueness of each person whom you meet and for the freedom of that person to be himself or herself. Love for others will be engendered only if you can trust in their basic goodness and inner beauty.

But the greater our awareness is of the indwelling presence of God in the deepest center of our being, the greater we will become conscious of this same divine, loving presence, surrounding and penetrating all other things. Gone are the anxious, aggressive moods to dominate each situation to satisfy our physical and psychic needs. A new global sense of God's presence is discovered in each human encounter as we push aside the veils of the externals to enter into the inner, loving presence of God. As we become freed from our false *ego*, the screaming lies and suspicious doubts about our own identity and that of others, we can remain humble and loving, gently looking into the eyes of each person encountered to see there the face of God, shining through as Love in the unique gift of the other person.

INNER COMMUNICATION

God has made us to enter into a deep intimacy with Him who is dwelling within us at all times. He dwells as a community of three Persons, Father, Son and Holy Spirit, all giving themselves in self-emptying to us in their uncreated energies flowing into our consciousness from within us by their indwelling presence. All too often we fail to grow in a listening to God within us because we have made God a very vengeful, legalistic God who will always remain extrinsic to us as a lawmaker. Such an enforcer of the law will not be intrinsic to us as a part of our true being.

To discover God as loving and intimately present within us, we are in need of a continued process of listening to His presence with greater attentiveness and consciousness or awareness. Prayer is the key that leads us to ever increasing levels of expanded consciousness of our oneness with God in love. Christian prayer through the faith, hope and love infused into us praying by the Spirit of Jesus Christ is an on-going process of discovering not only the abyss that separates the Absolute, all holy God from us sinners, but also of discovering the depths of oneness that exist between us and God in the very depths of our being. Growth in prayer is, therefore, a growth in awareness of God, especially as He lives and acts through His infinite love within us.

To enter into the inner reality of God's indwelling presence within you, you have need to leave the periphery, the noise, competition, all-absorbing anxieties and fears that militate against the silence and calm necessary for you to listen to God communicate Himself to you. This requires a certain amount of physical silence and tranquillity as well as a psychic silencing of your emotions, imagination, memory, intellect and will. But the greatest, most necessary silence that will allow you to love always in the presence of God, always listening and obeying God according to His communicated will is that silence that brings harmony between your spirit and God's Spirit. It is here that heart speaks to heart in the language of self-surrendering love.

GROWTH IN CONSCIOUS AWARENESS

As you move continually away from yourself as the center of your value system, you move in a continued "conversion" toward the indwelling God as your sole Center. Such a movement in listening to God's presence from within you admits of certain peak or threshold experiences. Jan Ruysbroeck, the 14th century Flemish mystic, teaches that the first level of breakthrough toward deeper interiority consists in the spiritual growth in the belief that the Trinity dwells within you and that, as often as you turn within and believe, you can expect to find God dwelling within you and loving you infinitely.

At times this spiritual awareness as an infusion of deeper faith, hope and love from God, quite unexpectedly comes upon you. It might be as you watch the ocean in storm or in peace, on a mountain top overlooking a beautiful sinking sunset in the west, in a moment of prayer in your bedroom or during a retreat. The suddenness of the experience shows that it is a gift from God that quickens you to a new level of awareness of the allness of God in your life.

There is also the medium of receiving that new gift of

awareness through deeper faith, hope and love that is quite
dependent upon you and your own activities to increase your
psychological consciousness by forming a new habit of
thought. The psychological element in this deeper awareness
comes about first by your realizing through reflection that
there are positive elements in your personhood that come
from God's loving goodness. It is important that you accept the
good qualities that God has placed within you, such as the
natural endowments, talents, skills and all the potentialities
that you feel surging from within the depths of your being
toward new and more enriching life. Whatever is good and
positive in you comes from God as a gift (Jm 1:17) and needs to
be affirmed and accepted with humility and gratitude by directing all good within you toward your Source, God Himself.

You must also be diligent to rid yourself of all distracting
thoughts and attachments of your heart toward any created
being, especially yourself. Here is a grave responsibility to
guard your senses, both exterior and interior, so as not to allow
the useless and "worldly" (i.e. whatever feeds your spirit of
self-absorption) to enter into your mind and carry you away
from union with God. "Happy the pure in heart; they shall see
God" (Mt 5:8).

But the most important activity on your part is that, as
often as you can, you have a free, spontaneous turning of your
will toward God so that your whole being is directed, body, soul
and spirit, in love to praise and glorify God.

LISTENING TO OTHERS IN LOVE

The paradox of true love toward the indwelling Trinity
within you as you listen to God the Father speak His word
through His Spirit of love is that such a listening allows you to
listen to the same God who speaks His Word in His Spirit in the
events of your daily life. As the Trinity brings you into a sense

of your "belonging," of being brought into the very family of the Trinity, this sense of unity gives you a new-founded sense of individuation. You know through this deep, abiding experience that you are being constantly loved by the three Divine Persons. You know yourself as an *I* loved by three Persons, each a *Thou*, in a *We* community.

Now you are capable of giving yourself to others through the Word that has been spoken within your heart. Your identity no one can take from you. You go into the broken, sordid, filthy world around you but you listen deeper to what the same Word that speaks you into your being is saying in this or that moment and event. God in His energies of love permeates every material atom of this universe. Everything that is happening around you is God gifting of Himself to you and the persons around you. You may be slighted, insulted, rejected, even hated by others. Still you stand firm and listen with an inner ear of love. You know, not only from whom you have come, but also from whom all things are coming and toward whom all things are moving.

You give up your mercurial, changing moods, attitudes and prejudices according to the whims and opinions of those around you. Yet you are humbly open as a loving servant to serve the deepest happiness of others. The *event* is what dynamically is being presented to you out of which God's Word is being brought to a new birth. By faith you can believe that God is coming out of this or that moment in a new reflection of glory. That this moment is unto His glory is what you are hearing. What is happening *now* is that God is speaking and you are listening. You go *into* this event to discover inside it what was already stored there. You enter into the given event to find God coming out of it (*evenire* in Latin) and in that moment there takes place the loving union of your will and that of God as they become one.

"Speak, Lord, your servant is listening" (1 S 3:10), is your constant outpouring of love in humble service to be used by God to bring forth new life in others. You learn to yield gently to God's loving presence in yourself so you can think and act as a whole, healed person. Aggressiveness against others disappears as you gently let the presence of God come forth from within you and from the depths of this given moment as you encounter those around you in love. Listening is the first step in true love, then loving action follows.

Chapter Ten

The Discipline of Inner Attentiveness

What we are beginning to see around us in our modern living is a return to discipline. Gross materialism and affluence, combined with the propaganda of TV commercials and instant success stories, have created the myth that you can become anyone you wish to be merely by wishing to do so. Naive college students felt they could become expert medical doctors or lawyers by over-indulging in drugs, alcohol, promiscuous sex without the discipline of hard work in study. Workers felt that unions would continuously gain for them more material benefits for less work. Men and women are disciplining their bodies by vigorous and consistent exercises and dieting. There is a return to discipline as a necessary means if one seriously wants to attain a desired end.

THE END OF LIFE

Jesus taught us the end of our Christian life. Yahweh had commanded His chosen people in the desert to love Him with their whole hearts and with all their strength (Dt 6:5). Jesus paraphrased this same command to be the summary of the end of our human life:

> You must love the Lord your God with all your heart, with all your soul, and with all your mind. This is the greatest and the

first commandment. The second resembles it: You must love
your neighbor as yourself. On these two commandments hang
the whole Law, and the Prophets also (Mt 22:37-40).

The greatest accomplishment or goal in our human existence is to love God perfectly in every thought, word and deed
and to love our neighbor as we would love ourselves. Whatever
else we do during our sojourn on this earth is subordinated to
this supreme end and should help us to attain it. But what
difficulties we encounter when we strive to place God as the
supreme center of all our inner motivations and values! As we
understand the greatness of God and His absolute beauty and
goodness in His infinite love for us, we will begin to understand ourselves on two levels of existence. We will see the areas
of darkness that rise up from within the depths of our hearts
that take on a force of aggressiveness as an enemy that attacks
us from within the very confines of our inner citadel. We will
also see our inner dignity to which God calls us and humbly we
will stretch out with great desire to put on the mind of Christ.

SIN IN MY MEMBERS

As you and I listen to the commands of God's Word, Jesus
Christ from within us, speaking them in continuity with His
revelation in Scripture and in church traditions, we strive to
fulfill them as faithfully as possible. We attentively listen to
God's inspirations and wishes expressed in the concrete details
of our state of life and the human situation in which we find
ourselves and we find even greater difficulties in being prompt
and generous to carry out God's wishes. From time to time we
are moved by the Spirit of love to express our returned love to
God in creative suffering that we spontaneously choose that
costs us a price in struggle and self-sacrifice and we find here,

even in the doing of generous deeds, the source of much self-centeredness and pride.

Jesus had told us of the necessity of being vigilant and attentive. "Therefore, you too must stand ready because the Son of Man is coming at an hour you do not expect" (Mt 24:44). We are to be vigilant like the five wise virgins who were found waiting when the bridegroom came (Mt 25:1-13). We are to purify our hearts from within for it is there that evil comes forth to make us unclean. "But the things that come out of the mouth come from the heart, and it is these that make a man unclean" (Mt 15:18).

He Himself went against His own will to embrace death out of love for the Father's will (Lk 22:43). And He preached the necessity of giving up a lower level of existence in order that new and more enriching life might come forth from the death to the former. "Anyone who finds his life will lose it; anyone who loses his life for my sake will find it" (Mt 10:39). "Unless a wheat grain falls on the ground and dies, it remains only a single grain; but if it dies, it yields a rich harvest. Anyone who loves his life loses it" (Jn 12:24-25).

St. Paul spoke for all of us when he described the inner forces within his very being that warred against him to destroy him and prevent him from doing any good.

> But I am unspiritual; I have been sold as a slave to sin. I cannot understand my own behavior. I fail to carry out the things I want to do, and I find myself doing the very things I hate. When I act against my own will, that means I have a self that acknowledges that the Law is good, and so the thing behaving in that way is not myself but sin living in me. The fact is, I know of nothing good living in me—living, that is, in my unspiritual self—for though the will to do what is good is in me, the performance is not, with the result that instead of doing the good things I want to do, I carry out the sinful things I do not

want. When I act against my will, then, it is not my true self
doing it, but sin which lives in me. . . . This is what makes me a
prisoner of that law of sin which lives inside my body. What a
wretched man I am! Who will rescue me from this body
doomed to death? Thanks be to God through Jesus Christ our
Lord! (Rm 7:14-25).

St. Paul knew the importance of disciplining his body in
order that he might run to win the crown in the race for
salvation (1 Cor 9:24-27). He strained ahead and never looked
back, all in order to do whatever would be necessary to gain the
"prize to which God calls us upwards to receive in Christ Jesus"
(Ph 3:14). He described the spiritual life in terms of a warfare,
a battle engaged against spiritual forces that are seeking his
destruction. God will grant us strength but we must resist the
cunning of the devil by taking up all God's armor (Ep 6:10-17).
And St. Peter strongly insists on the need for discipline against
the attacks of the enemy: "Be sober and watch well; the devil,
who is your enemy, goes about roaring like a lion, to find his
prey, but you, grounded in the faith, must face him boldly" (1
P 5:8-9).

EXPERIENCE OF DARKNESS

St. Augustine expressed what is our constant experience.
He desired, as we do, to love God with his whole heart; yet he
failed so often. In the 10th book of his *Confessions*, he conducts
an examination of conscience to discover whether he had
seriously offended God in the use of his five senses. When he
reaches the sense of smell he absolves himself that he has never
sinned in this matter, but he accurately observes: "That is my
judgment, but I could be mistaken, for there are in me those
lamentable darknesses I know so well and in the midst of them
the powers of my own soul that in me lie hidden from me. The
result is that when my mind of its own strength puts questions

to itself it does not feel that it can readily credit the answers that it gets. . . . Because what is in me is for the most part hidden from me unless it come forth and be manifested by experience."

You surely have often had the experience, not only of distractions during your busy day taking you away from God, your Center, but even when you were centered upon God, you found yourself rationalizing yourself into a position that was not totally freed from selfishness. Before you can speak or act in unity with God as your Center, you are in need to stand vigilant and attentive with disciplined detachment from self-centeredness to uproot anything that might take you away from living in a loving manner. The old self must be put to death and the new self allowed to come forth. This requires an inner revolution of the interior self, as St. Paul insisted. "Your mind must be renewed by a spiritual revolution so that you can put on the new self that has been created in God's way, in the goodness and holiness of the truth" (Ep 4:23-24). You are to bring every thought as prisoner, captured to be brought into obedience to Jesus Christ (2 Cor 10:5-6).

This is your striving to attain "purity of heart" that allows you to see God everywhere once you have put to death everything that keeps you locked inside of your inner darkness that has not yet been brought under the dominion of Christ the Lord. The early Christians of the desert called this inner attention *nepsis*. It comes from the Greek word *nepo* which refers to a mental equilibrium, a sobriety, an internal disposition of attention to the movement of the Spirit leading one to true discernment of how one should react to any given situation or in time of any temptation as befitting a child of so great a loving Father. Evagrius of the 4th century encourages Christians to so guard their mind that they place an inner sentinel or guard at the door of their consciousness. This guard is to stop each suggestion or thought and scrutinize it. "Are you for Christ or

against Him?" With courage and force the suggestion is re-
sisted at once if it seems to move the Christian away from
unselfish love of God and neighbor toward self-indulgence.

SELF-KNOWLEDGE

You become the desires that you entertain. You create the
world around you, at least the world that is important to you by
the thoughts that you value as important. Discipline over your
thoughts so that they are all submitted to the presence and the
love of Christ becomes the means for your entrance into true
freedom. But such freedom can be won only by a constant
battle over the powers of darkness that lie within you, in your
heart. The choice of whom you become lies within your power
through discipline that is permeated always by God's uncreated energies of love. God still challenges you to make your
choice as He did so long ago to His people:

> I set before you life or death, blessing or curse. Choose life,
> then so that you and your descendants may live, in the love of
> Yahweh your God, obeying his voice, clinging to him; for in
> this your life consists, and on this depends your long stay in the
> land which Yahweh swore to your fathers Abraham, Isaac and
> Jacob he would give them (Dt 30:19-20).

We know ourselves not only in the words and deeds that
enter into the world of history as soon as we have spoken or
acted, but we must come to know ourselves before words are
spoken and deeds done. We need to know who we can be by
"catching" the thoughts in their very origin as they arise within
our consciousness. Temptations are never in themselves evil or
wrong since Jesus was tempted in all things (Heb 4:15), yet He
never sinned. The masters of the spiritual life have always
insisted that we are to resist temptations in the very beginning
stage of the very suggestion arising from out of the dark areas
of our being. If we "dialogue" with it, the thought becomes

more appealing. Our reason can get into the act by presenting impelling motives why we should accept the suggestion and act on it. When we surrender repeatedly to such an enticing temptation that leads us away from true love we become captured and finally a habit is formed that destroys progressively our freedom as we continue to yield to the sinful impulse.

All Christians are called to be perfect as their Heavenly Father is perfect (Mt 5:48). All are called to live in love for God and neighbor. But this goal cannot be attained without the inner discipline of confronting with courage and constancy every thought and submitting it to the goal of every human life: does it make one more loving? Remaining in the presence of God is necessary to be centered on the Source and the End of all our strivings. But the discipline of examining each thought from within as it arises is something that only you and I can and must do if we are serious about attaining the goal: to live in love.

No one can give you this self-knowledge. You need to submit at each moment every movement from within to the guidance of God's Word dwelling within you. This is why being very conscious at all times of God's indwelling presence within you is so important. But the added step that brings you into the fruition of why you remain as centered as you can at all times lies in your disciplined accountability to put all thoughts under the sign of Christ.

But you know that in the heat of your activities you may not always have the concentration and the living faith to discern the delicate movements of the Holy Spirit. This is evident in all our lives daily. We do not grasp each situation as it begins to unfold in our consciousness to put it under the power of God's Word, Jesus Christ. For this reason I believe the following disciplined exercise is most important for you to grow in self-knowledge and inner healing of the failures and sins, the broken relationships of any given day.

God speaks His word to you at each moment of your daily life. This existential word should be in congruence with the words that He has spoken in Scriptures and in the Church's teachings that become normative of a good, Christian life and hence of what will make your life most successful and meaningful in the light of your ultimate goal in life. The secret of this exercise lies in your becoming transcendently present to God as you learn to listen with a gentle spirit to His judgment on who you are in the light of your daily thoughts, moods, actions and reactions. This is more than your mere self-analysis, but an operation of yours informed by God's illuminating Spirit.

Try doing this exercise at least each evening just before retiring for sleep and perhaps you can even find time to do it also at noon each day. Place yourself reverently in the presence of God by acts of faith, adoration, hope and love.

1. Begin by praising and thanking God for His innumerable gifts, those of a general and those of a specific nature received that day.

2. Beg Jesus to release His Spirit to enlighten you to see yourself as God sees you that day. How did you live this day according to the mind of God and the inner dignity to which God has called you?

3. Review the day, moment by moment, relationships with God, others, yourself, your moods, thoughts, omissions, hurts received and hurts you inflicted upon others. The good you did with God's grace and your cooperation. The need for amendment and healing.

4. Sorrow that heals. Picture Christ the Divine Physician touching you in any brokenness and healing you. See yourself becoming more healed and more whole.

5. Gift of the next day. Give God every thought, word and deed, joy and sorrow of the next day. Beg God to be present

and assist you to live in greater awareness of His indwelling presence and to bring every thought under His love.

PASSIONATE INDIFFERENCE

Teilhard de Chardin exhorts the modern Christian to reach a state of inner attentiveness to the loving presence of God within the individual and in the world around him or her. It is a sensitive turning to God within to see whether this or that thought is really in harmony with the Heavenly Father's will. It is not mere resignation to what happens within and outside of ourselves, but is a positive movement to direct our thinking, every thought as it begins to develop within our consciousness, toward God as the goal of all our striving. Such recollection of being centered upon God consciously in faith, hope and love and such inner self-activity of controlling your thoughts and bringing them under God's dominion go together. Recollection without inner vigilance and attentiveness is not enough to bring us into true wholeness and allow us to live constantly in loving oneness with God's will. Guarding your heart moves the initial act of love that prompted you to remain in the conscious presence of God to a deeper love, for it wishes not only to bring God's healing love into the dark areas of your being but you are desirous to have no thought but the thought of Jesus Christ.

Only in this way can you truly live constantly in love and be who you are in God's eternal designs. Only through this attentiveness within you over all your thoughts can you succeed in praying incessantly as St. Paul exhorts the early Christians: "Be happy at all times; pray constantly; and for all things give thanks to God, because this is what God expects you to do in Christ Jesus" (1 Th 5:16-18). Thus your will will become always one with God's will. This is how you can truly fulfill the end of your life: to love God with your whole heart, your whole soul, your whole mind and your strength and to love your neighbor as yourself.

Chapter Eleven

An Obeying Abandonment to the Indwelling Voice

When Christ preached His saving message to the multitudes, many applauded Him and wanted to be His followers. But when He began to spell out the conditions and the absoluteness of His demands that they would have to pay as the price of having a share with Him in His Kingdom, the crowds thinned out; even His twelve chosen apostles ran away and disowned Him when it came down to the bottom line.

> If anyone wants to be a follower of mine, let him renounce himself and take up his cross and follow me. For anyone who wants to save his life will lose it; but anyone, who loses his life for my sake and for the sake of the gospel, will save it (Mk 8:34-35).

All Christians would eagerly want eternal life. They would even want a deep, prayerful life that would allow them to walk always in the presence of God's love and power. But so many of us falter when Christ begins to make demands that threaten to put to death our false ego. Meister Eckhart, the 14th century Dominican German mystic, put it concretely:

> There are plenty to follow our Lord half-way, but not the other half. They will give up possessions, friends and honors, but it touches them too closely to disown themselves.

St. Ignatius of Loyola in his *Spiritual Exercises* describes three classes of Christians according to their will—set to follow

Christ generously or to make compromises. The first class are the *wishful* thinkers. Such followers of Christ want to be holy, but they never quite get around to taking the first necessary steps toward that goal. They recall the prayer of St. Augustine who in his *Confessions* prays to God that He might take away from him his carnal attachment to his concubine with whom he had been living for 14 years, but then he whispers in fear that God might hear his prayer: "But, Lord, not yet!"

The second class wants holiness and does take half-measures to arrive at the end. Such a Christian tends to rationalize himself/herself into an accommodated following of Christ. Such a person determines what God is asking and what the individual is willing to accept and also what the individual will not accept. A filter system is set up to hear from God only what the individual wishes to hear and to give up or to do whatever is in keeping with his/her convenience.

The third class is the *magnanimous* Christian in whom there is only one supreme magnificent obsession: God. God can ask anything of this person and there is promptitude, generosity and total surrender in love to carry through God's will. "Speak, Yahweh, your servant is listening" (1 S 3:10). Mary, the Mother of God, is the perfect example of such total obeying abandonment to God's wishes: "I am the handmaid of the Lord; let what you have said be done to me" (Lk 1:38). This is a process of growing ever more loving in response to God's infinite love toward the individual, since love ultimately consists in the gift of self to please the one loved.

TRUE LOVE OBEYS

True love is always self-emptying in loving service toward the one loved. Obedience to Christ is the index of our love for Him and of our loving union with Him. While reading the early Fathers of the desert, I have often been impressed by the fact that the one work they assigned to all Christians, regardless of their state of life, is to observe in loving obedience the commands of Christ. But this is only because such athletes for Christ understood the true nature of love as self-surrender in obedience to Christ.

We hear from Christ Himself that, if we truly love Him, we will keep His word "and my Father will love him, and we shall come to him and make our home with him" (Jn 14:23). Keeping Christ's word, for Christians, should be more than the observance of the ten commandments. It goes even beyond observing all that Jesus commanded in the New Testament teachings.

It comes down to a state of listening to the indwelling Christ, as He, through His Spirit, reveals to you the mind of the Father in each event. But listening must move to obedience for only in self-surrender in order to please the one you love is true love discovered and actualized. The end of the incarnation is precisely that God's divine life may be restored within your inner being by Jesus Christ entering within your spiritual faculties by the divine uncreated energies of love. You should desire hungrily to possess this inner presence of Jesus Christ as light in a more conscious, unifying way. You burn within yourself to hear His voice. But what transforms your life into a godly life of living in love for others in the unity of all things in Christ is your passion to allow God's Word to be done in your life through your perfect submission in obedience to His will.

DEGREES OF LOVING RESPONSE

For you there is no greater joy than to seek out and do willingly the will of the Heavenly Father. The secret of a truly happy and successful human life is gauged by your seeking, as Jesus always did in His earthly life, to please the Heavenly Father in all things, in every thought, word and deed. It is a

basic human understanding that if you love someone, you will
"die" to your own wishes and live to please the other. You will
wait on the wishes of that person and consider it a joy and a
privilege to "do" anything that would bring pleasure and happiness to that person.

Thus true love of God is not proved by words, no matter
how much you may say, "Lord, Lord," but solely by deeds, by
observing the will of God.

> If you keep my commandments
> you will remain in my love,
> just as I have kept my Father's commandments
> and remain in his love (Jn 15:10).

This is never a humiliating submission before a powerful,
austere God, but a filial surrender to a loving Father whose
loving activities surround you from all sides at all times. Doing
His will is the source of your greatest joy. Because God is
supreme and the sovereign cause of all that happens, it is
justice that demands obedience to God's will. All inanimate
creatures and all plants and animals *must* obey God's will. Only
we human beings can freely return the gift of our being. This is
why we become who we have been destined to be by God's love.
We reach our unique identity in God's love only when we
respond to that love in a process of continued self-giving in
love. But this self-giving and response to do the will of God
admits of many degrees of generosity in obedience. Our response will depend, not on how much God loves us for His love
is infinite, but rather on how much we become aware of His
immense, personalized love for us, manifested through Jesus
Christ in His Spirit.

OBEYING THE COMMANDS OF GOD

In His earthly life Jesus strove always to keep the commandments of the Heavenly Father. At times, especially in His

death, Jesus saw the command of the Father as something very demanding. Yet He answered always out of love: ". . . not my will, but thine be done" (Lk 22:42). If we experience a bit of God's love, we will show that degree of our love in return. The first level of generosity and love-giving consists in our willingness to obey God's voice as we see it commanding us to do what is essential in order that we may not break our communication with God by placing ourselves as supreme over God. He alone is supreme to command us under justice to obey or lose eternal life.

But in the life of Christ we see also that there were whole areas of decisions and choices that seemed to have been made very spontaneously, sometimes with reflection, sometimes in deep, silent prayer, sometimes with a movement into His heart, there to listen to the Father speak His love for Him and speak also what constituted in the concrete event of that moment the wish of the Father to be accomplished with love by His Son. This embraced the whole area of His seeking not merely to obey the commands of the Father but in all things to see through the delicate whisperings of the Spirit of love to do the slightest, manifested wish of the Father. A command is different from a wish even though both come from the same person we love.

It requires from Jesus, as from us, greater love, delicacy and discernment to be attentive interiorly to seek what is the wish of the Father in this or that circumstance of life rather than merely to fulfill His commands. Such a level of obedience is obtained by inner discipline to turn into the inner center of our being and there meet God in His "awful immediacy," to quote the Quaker, Thomas Kelly. As Jesus experienced His living and loving Father bursting over His consciousness through the delicate manifestations of the Spirit, He was propelled back into the heart of the Father to surrender in total gift of Himself to do whatever the Father was wishing of Him.

You and I show more love in obeying the will of the Father in seeking to do at all times whatever we sensitively see at this moment to be the expression of the Father's wish. You must be convinced that, in spite of your inner darkness and selfishness that still lurk within you, you can by the promise of Jesus and the outpouring of His Spirit, discern what the Father is wishing you to do in any given moment. Jesus promised to send His Spirit to His followers in order that that Spirit would teach them all about Jesus (Jn 14:25-27). The Spirit would lead them to complete truth (Jn 16:12-15). That same Spirit is promised by Jesus to be with you always if you only ask and seek Him from the Father (Lk 11:9-13).

St. Paul urges you to know the will of God through the release of the Spirit: "And do not be thoughtless but recognize what is the will of the Lord . . . be filled with the Spirit" (Ep 5:17-18). You need not fear that you may not have that Spirit without whom there can be no discernment of what would be the wish of the Father in the concrete details of a given moment, since your very body is a temple of the indwelling Spirit (1 Cor 3:16, 6:19). The Spirit of God's great love dwells within you (Rm 8:9) and will surely lead you into all truth through right discernment if you are only sincere enough to rely on Jesus' promise that He will release His Spirit to keep you from all error and sin.

CREATIVE SUFFERING

The greatest level of obedience in love is what I term "creative suffering." This is the highest level of human freedom in which one seeks to please the Heavenly Father by obeying the Spirit of love who does not indicate any specific command or wishes of the Father but who moves the individual Christian to an ardent response of love to create a symbol through offering a sacrifice entailing personal suffering that costs a price in order to "enflesh" that movement of love. This requires a going beyond but also an exact fulfillment of the commands and the expressed wishes of the Father.

We have all experienced this spontaneous movement in freedom to do something for a friend whom we love dearly. With no expression on the part of our friend as to what he or she wished, we strove to create a symbol of our love. The effectiveness of that symbol and the actualization of our hidden love in an "enfleshment" in a concretely expressed, material action lay in the "cost" in terms of personal suffering that we were willing to endure out of love for that friend.

Jesus, who had experienced in His human consciousness the love of the Father as no other person on the face of the earth had, sought to please His Father.

> He who sent me is with me, and has not left me to myself, for I always do what pleases him (Jn 8:29).

Creative suffering is no obligation. Jesus freely, spontaneously improvised ways to act out His surrender in perfect love back to the Father for the perfect love He had received from Him, the source of His being. Many of the humiliations during His trials and in His dying moments on the cross Jesus bore meekly as He interiorly wished to give Himself and empty Himself more completely by "dispossessing" Himself totally in order that His Father might be all in all. Only one who has deeply loved can understand how one, not in a sickly masochistic way, but in the healthiest, human way, can actually accept and seek sufferings, more and more, in order that love for God can grow more intensely. The martyrs down through the centuries have understood this universal law of love.

Such a level of generosity and obedience to God is dependent upon how deeply we experience the exuberance and cascading love of God flowing over us at all times. For one not experiencing this flaming love of God such suffering is excessive and irrational. St. Paul wanted to be "co-crucified" with

Christ so that Christ would live totally in him and he would live no longer merely he himself (Gal 2:20). He rejoiced in his sufferings for he wanted to be crucified with Christ Jesus, bearing in his body the marks of His passion. "All I want is to know Christ and the power of his resurrection and to share his sufferings by reproducing the pattern of his death. That is the way I can hope to take my place in the resurrection of the dead" (Ph 3:10-11).

Can you and I really want sufferings? Can we deliberately seek sufferings, especially when we find it so difficult to accept those sufferings that come "honestly" into our lives through active or passive diminishments of living in our human situation? We do know the free spontaneity that the Spirit stirs up from within our hearts from time to time to perform an act that costs us a price in personal self-denial, all in order, not to seek suffering for its own sake, but rather to flesh out our desire to please the Father and to return His great love. Such obedience, not to an expressed command or wish from God, but to a movement of the Spirit of love, occurs from time to time and grows out of your readiness to be sensitive to the indwelling Christ and to surrender to what His Spirit is revealing to you in the concrete circumstances of your daily living as that which would be the wish of the Father for you at that time.

BECOMING OBEDIENT

We never are totally obedient, therefore, in a static condition to do the will of the Father. Jesus had to grow in wisdom and knowledge and grace before God and man (Lk 2:52). So you and I are to grow into greater and greater obedience as we become more aware of God's infinite self-giving within us at the center of our being. And you begin this long process in growing in loving obedience by first believing that this is the end of your life, as seen imaged in the earthly life of Jesus and in the lives of the great saints. You have been made by God ultimately for God, that you should love Him with your whole heart, your whole soul and with all your actualized strength as you cooperate with the Spirit of Jesus to become a loving child of God, obedient in all things. Thus you return love for love and become a sharer in such love of His own divine nature (2 P 1:4).

The next step is to begin obeying God in this present moment with the love that you possess for God. Love begets love, and obedience out of love is the way love is engendered. You cannot seek to love God through creative suffering unless you have learned well how to obey God in His clear and evident commands and then to move on to embrace at each moment that which the Spirit reveals to you in your purity of heart and honest sincerity to be the wish of the Father in that given circumstance.

In each moment as you willingly wish to love God through obedience to His holy will you seek to render your motive of loving by obeying as explicitly as possible. "Lord, Thy will be done." "Father, I wish to direct this thought, action, word unto your infinite glory out of love for you."

The third step deals with our failures when we catch ourselves having turned away from God, our Center, and seeing that we were acting out of a "carnal" mind and not with the mind of Christ, to please the Father. Humbly acknowledge your diffusion and scatteredness and beg God's strength that you may try again in love to be more faithful to God who is always faithful to you.

The fourth step is most important as a continued stage that takes on a habitual attitude of mind. It has often been cited as a slogan: "Let go; let God." Rooted firmly within yourself at your center, God, you know that He is your strength. In Him you can do all things precisely because He is continually within you and strengthening you by His love.

Drop all Pelagianism, which is a heresy that teaches you can do it yourself without God's help. Become a child of God and realize that, although you are to cooperate freely with God, He is within you with an infinite power and love. "... and you have in you one who is greater than anyone in this world" (1 Jn 4:4).

ABANDONMENT

As you let go of your own control over yourself and God, you find yourself progressively abandoning yourself to let God have complete freedom to do with you whatever He wishes. This is a movement of grace that admits of many degrees and manifestations. It is not a static relationship to God nor is it a passive surrendering of all activities and desires on your part. It is the unfolding of the infusion of the Holy Spirit's gifts of deep faith in the Father's immense love for you, made manifest in Christ and that love is intimately going on in the depths of your being. From such faith you grow in confident trust or hope to let go of yourself.

Such trust leads you to childlike love that is an obeying abandonment. St. Therese of Lisieux describes for us in simple language what such loving abandonment meant for her:

> I have now no longer any desire except that of loving Jesus unto folly. Yes, it is love alone that attracts me. I no longer desire suffering nor death, and yet, I love both. I have desired them for a long time. I have had suffering and I have come close to dying. . . . Now, abandonment is my only guide. I can no longer ask ardently for anything except that God's will may be perfectly accomplished in my soul.

Abandonment is to live out your Christian Baptism by passing over through filial trust in God's infinite goodness from self-containment or self-possession to surrender yourself completely according to God's will. St. Francis de Sales writes that it is a true death to whatever we may wish or desire in order to abandon ourselves totally to the good pleasure of Divine Providence.

Such an obeying abandonment, flowing from a progressive growth in love for God, is rooted in the unshakeable conviction that all things lie under God's power and that He wills only out of His nature that is *love*. God cannot will anything out of any motive less than His desire to share His goodness with us human beings. His will is always turned toward ultimate good and our own supreme happiness. If it is true, as St. Paul says, "What God wants is for you to be holy" (1 Th 4:3), then all that falls under His guiding Providence ought to benefit us unto our eternal good and happiness.

If the love of God within you begets love as your response toward God, then abandonment is perfect obedience in the great élan of love toward the Heavenly Father that contains all other virtues. Its essence is a renunciation of all self-centeredness in order, out of love for God, to do what is perceived by the mind, enlightened by grace, to be the will of God. It is a total gift of yourself as you, in your human situations, seek to live according to the mind of God. Love is the key word in abandonment.

But when have you loved God sufficiently? Abandonment admits therefore of a continued process of self-surrender as you grow in greater love of God. St. Bernard insists that the measure in which we love God is to love Him without measure so that "once love has taken hold of the heart it carries all before it and renders captive all other affections."

EXTENT OF SURRENDER

Abandonment extends in its pure form to touch anything and everything of the past, present and future. How difficult it is to let go of your worries and anxieties stemming from your past. Even to let go of the joys of the past with detachment is most difficult. We tend to hold on to both the dark and the light of the past. The future, however, looms before you as exciting and at the same time foreboding. But it is this present moment that dances before your dreamy eyes with ever-changing forms, lovable and desirable, fearful and not wanted.

Teilhard de Chardin encourages us to have a "passionate indifference" toward all that has happened, is happening and will happen in the future. It is a mental state of holding yourself open to move freely toward whatever God's will indicates, in spite of any natural inclination or affection to the contrary. The love of God through His Spirit dwelling intimately within you has purified your centering away from yourself to become totally centered upon God and whatever would please Him. You refuse to act upon mere natural drawing or desire without placing your deliberative will under loving submission to whatever God may wish. Objects of such passionate indifference can be all temporal things that touch your well-being of body and mind. It would extend to prosperity or adversity, riches or poverty, individual and public calamities, health or sickness, life or death, reputation, honors or humiliations. It embraces also all spiritual goods, the life of grace, practice of virtues, failures and sins, temptations, consolations and aridities, trials and desolation.

And yet we are not feelingless or mindless beings. We are not puppets pulled to action by a Divine Puppeteer. We have been created, not as automatons, but as human beings with intellect and will. True love is possible and hence perfect obedience to the Divine Voice within is attained only with our cooperation. St. Augustine, who preached so eloquently the harmonious interaction of grace and man's cooperation in loving faith and hope, wrote: "He that created thee without thy knowledge will not save thee without thy consent."

It is clear from Jesus' teaching in the Gospels that we must strive to do God's will at all times, never being anxious and over-solicitous about anything else. Still He insists on our need to cooperate and do all God would wish us to do to obtain what we believe is according to God's will. He also insists that we pray to the Heavenly Father. Does true abandonment and perfect obedience to do God's will permit our desiring and praying for any concrete wished object on our part? We are encouraged to go to prayer for discernment to listen to God's commands and wishes to be expressed to us.

If in prayer, we see that we desire to pray for health in order to work for God's greater glory, this intention in prayer is effecting what our abandonment seeks to accomplish—to do more perfectly what will redound to God's greater glory.

We trust that God will provide for what we are to eat and put on but that means someone has to prepare the food and put the clothing on us. God will provide us with health but it may mean an operation and a stay in the hospital. We can pray and trust God will provide us with a job but His will directs us to knock on doors and seek employment. Parents must love their children but they must in the concrete circumstance of the now moment make efforts to correct them when they are in need of such.

God is truly to be found in a trusting abandonment to His holy will, but His will demands that we exercise prudence in doing all we can do to promote God's will. Part of God's order and our loving obedience is that we do all that depends on us. What God wishes in our obeying abandonment to His loving providence is that we avoid all excessive solicitude and anxiety in seeking things other than the Kingdom of God.

FRUIT OF OBEYING ABANDONMENT

The chief fruit of such abandonment to seek always God's holy will is that God becomes sovereign in our lives. Obstacles to grace stemming from our selfishness and attachment to our

own will are removed. This brings a deep and tender intimacy
with God.

You experience a continued growth in simplicity and freedom that approaches what Jesus experienced who centered
His whole earthly life on doing only the will of His Father.
Inordinate attachments and passions are cut out from your
life. The words of St. Paul become yours, for neither death nor
life, no created thing "can ever come between us and the love
of God made visible in Christ Jesus our Lord" (Rm 8:39).
Constancy and equanimity become the effects of your being
rooted in the unchangeable love of God. Your whims and
selfish feelings have no power now to determine your attitudes
and ways of acting, since you seek at all times only God's will.

God has become truly your Center. Grounded in such
stability, you enjoy peace and joy that no one can ever take
from you. God rules you. You will not want anything else
(Ps 23). And this brings you into that truth called humility.
Love and humility go hand in hand. One cannot exist without
the other. Abandonment destroys self-centeredness and
humility makes you "God-blinded," intoxicated with God's
love. Your values now change and you live in spirit and in
truth. You know yourself as nothing, absolutely nothing without God. Yet you know yourself as the beautiful gift that God
has created to be a receptacle that is emptied but to be filled
with God's goodness, in the words of St. Irenaeus of the 2nd
century.

Such is the result of living interiorly in the daily experience of God's infinite love for you. You live to serve God and,
strangely, as you lose your life and abandon yourself totally to
God's loving care, you discover your true self gradually emerging as a loving child, one with Christ, the only begotten Son of
the Father, living passionately to glorify the Father and experiencing at the same time your full nature and happiness in

loving, surrendering obedience where love and humility and abandonment all become ultimately one in your daily experience.

Chapter Twelve

Doing All Things In Love

A pilgrim in the Middle Ages paused before the cathedral of Chartres that was under construction. He watched a worker cutting a figure out of stone and asked him: "What are you doing?" I am sculpturing, evidently." The pilgrim moved to another worker who was doing the same type of work: "What are you doing?" I am earning a living," was the answer he received. He asked a third worker doing the same work: "What are you doing?" The worker answered: "I am building a cathedral!"

You no doubt have worked much in your life and will continue to spend a good deal of your time in hard work. Why do you work? Is it only to earn a living? But then why live? Is it only eventually to die? Why we work and how we work indicate what our idea is, not only of ourselves and of God, but also indicate whether our work humanizes us through the love generated for others in our efforts to work for them or whether it makes us more selfish and less human. The more transcendent and ultimate in concern can be our every thought, word and deed, the greater is our human growth. It is this that is the measure not only of our love for God and neighbor, but also of God's very own uncreated energies of love working in us and through us to fulfill His eternal plan.

A NEW VISION NEEDED

Through a Platonism that has run through Western Christianity, we have dichotomized God from His material creation. We tend, at least in our thinking and praying, to place God spatially outside of the material world, *up there*. The material world around us then does not become a *diaphanous* point in which we can encounter God as actively working and giving Himself to us by His uncreated energies of love precisely in the very creative work that we do in a oneness of wills with Him.

Work in such an outmoded view sees human work as a punishment for sin. It is true that human beings sinned and brought evil into this world. When man turned away from God's invitation to work in loving harmony to bring forth the material world into a greater oneness that would reflect God's loving oneness with all His created world, work became no longer a joyful, creative process with God as a prayerful worship and adoration. Human beings found themselves alienated from the created world around them. Sin separated man from man, from nature around him and even alienated his own powers within his very own being.

The account in *Genesis* of man's attitude toward work is told in mythopoetic terms:

> Accursed be the soil because of you.
> With suffering shall you get your food from it
> every day of your life.
> It shall yield you brambles and thistles,
> and you shall eat wild plants.
> With sweat on your brow
> shall you eat your bread,
> until you return to the soil,
> as you were taken from it (Gn 3:17-19).

When God created the material world and commissioned man to be creative and fruitful in developing the world's potential for good that would easily reflect God's goodness and love, He meant all parts to be coordinated into a whole, into a dancing harmony. We human beings, alone created by God with intellect and will and the power to know God's love and return that love by our life of creative work, were given stewardship over the riches of the material world. "Be fruitful, multiply, fill the earth and conquer it. Be masters of the fish of the sea, the birds of heaven and all living animals on the earth . . . God saw all he had made and indeed it was very good" (Gn 1:28-31).

We know only too well the effects of sin upon our material world and our attitude toward work. Man has become the center of work and no longer God. Nature around man is an enemy to be conquered and exploited, raped of all its richness in order to supply man greater power that spells greater sense pleasures to himself. Through the deductive methods of science, we have developed a way to invent tools to help us in the conquest of nature. We can predict the way things should happen. But along with this ability we have determined our own values that usually are individualistic and not communal, exploitative and not sharing riches with those who have not as much as we.

Man's ideas of what is good for the entire world have produced water and air pollution; pillage of mineral resources; the increasing list of extinct or endangered species of birds and animals; the far-reaching effect of pesticides; the wanton dumping of industrial chemicals on land and sea; the overwhelming accumulation of waste, garbage and junk, all building up to an apocalyptic crisis. We live in fear and each day brings greater individual fear of safety for one's self against criminals or diseases and greater national fear through nuclear armament. We were made out of God's love for love, to live in harmony with God and neighbor, but everywhere we look we see the darkness of fears, anxieties and greater isolation from others and from God as man enters into his selfish world of nothingness.

A NEW CREATION

But God did not forsake His material creation that He always saw as good. Into this broken world He sent His Son who took upon Himself our materiality, was tempted in all things, save sin (Heb 4:15), in order to reestablish the initial harmony through His infinite love in dying for us human beings. "God dealt with sin by sending his own Son in a body as physical as any sinful body, and in that body God condemned sin" (Rm 8:3). Christ condemned sin in the flesh through His death and resurrection whereby He passed gloriously from the state of flesh (*sarx*) to that of spirit (*Pneuma*). Once God spoke definitively His Word in His Suffering Servant, Jesus, on the cross, the risen Jesus Christ was able to pour out into our hearts His Spirit of love (Rm 5:5). By His resurrection the bodies of all of us and the whole material universe would be given the possibility to be re-oriented to God. We are now able in the light of God's infinite love for us as proved by Jesus dying unto the last drop of blood to break our self-centeredness and move into a new life in God. It opens up to us also the ability to work now with the infinite, uncreated energies of God's love to create a new world of all things in oneness through love in Christ.

Now Jesus is the New Adam and the Lord of the universe. He is marvelously inserted through His resurrection into this material world and capable of directing it into a unity in His risen body. He invites us to become His ambassadors and reconcilers of the whole world (2 Cor 5:17-20) through our cooperation in creative work with Christ to make all things one in Him.

The Greek Fathers use two words to convey how the entire material world not only can become for us a diaphany, a shining through of God's immanent presence as love, but it can also become the *place* where we co-create with God a new Jerusalem. The first word, *symbiosis*, means literally "a life with." The other word, *synergy*, means "a working with." Here we have the elements of moving into deeper faith that God is one with us in the life of love that Christ has brought us in His Spirit. As we become aware of God's immediacy to us, living more intimately to ourselves than we ourselves, in the words of St. Augustine, we can also believe easily that God is also immanently present in all things. We easily learn to believe that God is not only present and close to us, immanently present within us and sharing His live with us, but that He wishes to share His life with the world around us.

We move from this awareness of a life with God to the natural step of working in love with God as we discover that God's immanent presence within us and the world is one of active, loving work to bring about a "communion" so that in the very creative work that we do in love with Him we can bring about the initial harmony and oneness with all things.

PRESENCE OF GOD

How can we ultimately work always and still contemplate God in all things and in our very work grow in greater love toward God and neighbor? How can we break out of the out-moded spiritual vision that separates prayer and work, the sacred and the secular worlds, spirit and matter? The *first* stage is to become aware of God's divine immanence close to us, within us and within all material things that surround us. This awareness admits of great intensity and comes about in an unending process through God's gift of faith and our own desire to possess this inner knowledge or intuition to ever increasing degrees.

We push ourselves, not by any intellectual process or even by our own imagining how God is present, to live joyfully in the presence of God in all things. "Seek Yahweh and his strength, seek his face untiringly; remember the marvels he has done, his wonders, the judgments from his mouth" (Ps 105:4-5). Those who exist in the state called Heaven walk ever in His loving presence. They see God face to face (1 Cor 13:12) and never can lose Him, while we still must glimpse Him now darkly as in a mirror. This is an imperfect, shadowy knowledge, "but then I shall know as fully as I am known" (1 Cor 13:12).

So in ever increasing faith as we seek to live in God's presence, we can enter more fully into His love. "I keep Yahweh before me always, for with him at my right hand nothing can shake me . . . you will reveal the path of life to me, give me unbounded joy in your presence, and at your right hand everlasting pleasures" (Ps 16:8-9, 11).

God is ever present to us. He never forgets us as we try never to forget His loving presence. He is within us at all times, for in Him we live and move and have our being (Ac 17:28).

> Where could I go to escape your spirit?
> Where could I flee from your presence?
> If I climb the heavens, you are there,
> there too, if I lie in Sheol.
> If I flew to the point of sunrise,
> or westward across the sea,
> your hand would still be guiding me,
> your right hand holding me (Ps 139:7-10).

God's presence within you and within all of nature around you cannot be argued to, but only surrendered to. Moses "held to his purpose like a man who could see the Invisible"

(Heb 11:27). So too you have eyes to pierce through your very own being and find God there dwelling within you at all times. You have eyes of faith to pierce through the events of your day to find God present within, bringing all things unto goodness because you now believe as St. Paul encourages you to do: "We know that by turning everything to their good, God cooperates with all those who love him, with all those that he has called according to his purpose" (Rm 8:28).

SURRENDERING PRESENCE
TO THE WORKING OF GOD

The *second* degree of presence to God's immanent presence in all things is not only to "see" Him there by faith, but you are to surrender to Him as you contemplate God actively holding all things together (Ac 17:28). Such an added faith convinces you that if God is present, He is love and His love is *action*. We know in our daily lives that love is proved by deeds. When we love anyone, we wish to work to act out our love by symbolic actions of our surrender of self to the other. This step of God's presence leads us interiorly to Him at the heart of all matter as uncreated energies of love. God is not merely present in all things, holding them in their being, but He is also continuously creating the world. God is dynamically in motion as He creates the world, but through human beings like you and me. It is for us to recognize by deep faith that God is actively creating in all circumstances, be they our active works or simply events that happen to us as we passively accept them.

The *third* level, therefore, of being present to God is to accept, not with blind resignation, but with loving abandonment to His energetic love in each moment, all that is happening to you right now. As you go through your day you become very much aware that the divine presence of God, like rays of the sun, glows within the cosmos. In the very work that you are doing, you can make contact with God and be in a constant state of worship, adoration and self-surrender to God as you see God not merely working in each event but working in love so that you lovingly kiss His hand at each moment as He gives Himself to you in that event.

The *fourth* stage of becoming present to God's all-presence is to believe by child-like faith through Scripture and the teaching of the Church that God is creating and is loving in His creation, that He is a transforming, deifying, loving energy that is moving you and through you the entire material world into a oneness. We have already seen that God is love by nature and therefore is emptying Himself out in self-gift to us so that we might share not merely His created gifts, but that we might share His very own life and *being*. The Kingdom of God is being fashioned by God and man working together to re-capitulate all of creation. This is a process that the early Fathers called *theosis* or divinization.

Now you can see that your *symbiosis* or life with God leads you into a sharing with His energies of love as you enter into a *synergy*, a working with God to fulfill God's beginning creation. This is your greatest dignity, to be called God's "recapitulator," to bring all things into harmony and oneness through your contribution to the creative power of God.

But your faith through God's revelation leads you to the *fifth* level of presence to God's intimate presence in all things. Not only do you wish to work to bring harmony into the world by a loving cooperation with the mind of God, but now you strive by deepest faith to realize that what you are building is the very Body of Christ. God is no longer merely the *One-on-high* or the *Within* of all things, but He is also the *Beyond*. At this stage of your being present to God in your actions and works done out of love and in union with God's actions, you realize that you are called by God to fashion out of the materiality of this universe the Body of Christ. You believe in St. Paul's vision that ultimately: "There is only Christ: he is everything and he is in everything" (Col 3:11).

BUILDING THE BODY OF CHRIST

To become your true self you must more and more transcend the limitations imposed by your false self to stretch forth in creative, loving actions to live for others. In your loving union through your work you discover your true self in greater degrees of awareness, only to give yourself more completely to live for others in purer love. The more you can act with full consciousness and reflection, the more you "humanize" yourself, unleashing the spiritual powers that enable you to transcend the material, the limited, the particular and pass over to the realm of the enduring and limitless spirit. When you can by faith realize that your loving action is having an eternal effect upon the entire universe and is bringing somewhat God's plan into fulfillment, then you can throw yourself into that action, whatever it may be, and find that it is unifying prayer.

This is not to deny that you have need to come aside from your many actions in a material universe and find in sacred moments of retirement the immanent life of the Trinity of the Father, Son and Holy Spirit within you. It means also that you open yourself to the sacramental life of the Church, especially in the celebration of the Divine Liturgy as you join yourself in union with fellow Christians to perform religious acts that have God as your explicit object of adoration.

Still the major portion of your time in the modern world setting is spent in action, not necessarily physical labor, but in absorbing immersion in material things of the world. And never before has the human race an access to a larger array of creatures. You cannot choose all of them. You must choose some, to the exclusion of others. You cannot be a medical doctor and a lawyer and a farmer all at the same time. The more you choose your work according to the charisms that God has given you and in an intimate *I-Thou* relationship you work with God to bring forth the completion of His world, the more you liberate yourself and become truly free in your true being that was always oriented to be made according to God's own image and likeness (Gn 1:26).

God does not create for death or annihilation, but He gives you life and a universe teeming with millions of fellow creatures in order to help Him achieve His one, united plan. God is not like a jealous Zeus, punishing Prometheus for having given the gift of fire to man. All created beings are God's gifts to be used and developed by thinking persons so that eventually, in St. Paul's words, "creation itself would be delivered from its slavery to corruption, to enjoy the freedom that comes with the glory of the children of God. For we know that all creation groans and travails in pain until now" (Rm 8:21-22).

THE CHURCH

At the center of this created universe your Christian faith presents to you the risen Jesus Christ. Not only do you believe that through Christ your total person, body, soul and spirit relationships, will be joined to the resurrectional life of the living Savior, but your faith expresses itself in the hope that the whole cosmos will be transfigured into a "new creation." It is the glorified Christ who associates Himself as mediator in bringing the universe to its appointed completion.

St. Paul pictures Christ bringing all under subjection to Him so that He can bring it back to His Heavenly Father, "in order that God may be everything to everyone and everything" (1 Cor 15:28). In Jesus Christ, God the Father has destined that the fullness of the whole universe should dwell. He is reconciling, recapitulating, leading back to His Heavenly

Father the entire created universe, but one fulfilled and actuated in its fullness by being one with Christ (Col 1:15-20).

God's will is "to gather all creation both in heaven and on earth under one head, Christ" (Ep 1:10). Christ has complete primacy and dominion over the cosmic universe through His death and resurrection. "He (God) has subjected every single thing to his authority and has appointed him sovereign head of the Church which is truly his body, the complement of him who fills all members with all graces" (Ep 1:22-23). The Body of Christ is His Church (Ep 5:23-30). He is united to His followers as the head is united with all the members of the body.

The Church is not opposed to the world but it guarantees its only completion. Your work, when it is consciously done by you as a living member of the Body of Christ, in submission to your Head, Jesus Christ, partakes of an ecclesial act. You are building the Body of Christ. The ecclesial function of giving God's life to individuals extends beyond the limitations of the visible hierarchical Church.

A stone tossed into a placid lake produces ripples that spread out into continuous concentric circles, moving from the center until the circles touch the landed shore. The Church is the center from which grace, God's life, goes out to touch all parts of the world. At this center, generating the outward movement, are the sacraments, chiefly the Eucharist, which gives us the Body-Person of Jesus Christ as physically present and acting among us as our Head. The circles spread out, becoming larger until they almost merge, but even here the impact of Christ, the Pantocrator, the Lord of the Universe, continues to be felt. Thus you have the sacraments and Christ's living Word through the Church's preaching, added to your own human activities informed by grace, spreading out beyond the physical limitations of the visible Church to make Christ's grace manifest to the world in an incarnated form.

The world is basically religious and oriented toward the explicit, full life of Christ found only in the Church, in His Body of which He is the Head, the Life-Giver. You work upon the matter you touch in your daily activities, much as a priest takes bread and wine and offers them up to God before the Spirit of love transforms them into the Body of Christ. Now nothing you do is merely "secular" or "profane." Nothing of your working activities in a world of great movement and multiplicity, confusion and chaos, can take you away from your oneness with Christ your Head as you offer your service to Him so that He can pour His Spirit of love through your humble actions and, like Mary, the Mother of Christ, you can help to bring forth to this world the Body of Christ.

Teilhard de Chardin beautifully describes how you can unite the secular and the sacral:

> Try, with God's help, to perceive the connection—even physical and natural—which binds your labor with the building of the Kingdom of Heaven. . . . Never, at any time, "whether eating or drinking," consent to do anything without first of all realizing its significance and constructive value in *Christo Jesu*, and pursuing it with all your might. This is not simply a commonplace precept for salvation: it is the very path to sanctity for each man according to his state and calling. For what is sanctity in a creature if not to cleave to God with the maximum of his strength? And, what does that maximum cleaving to God mean if not the fulfillment—in the world organized around Christ— of the exact function, be it lowly or eminent, to which that creature is destined both by nature and supernature? (*The Divine Milieu*, pp. 35-36).

TRANSCENDING ACTION

People at different levels of personality development and prayer life express the inner core of being where their outflowing energy approximates closely the divine act of creation.

A mother working patiently to form her child, a Peace Corps worker in the heart of Africa, a religious or lay person teaching a class, all have experienced what it means to transcend the empirical, external *eros*-determinations in order to penetrate deep within themselves, and, at the core of their being, to find the spark of divine creativity which enables them to give themselves in unselfish love for others.

This is true liberation, a real expansion, a resurrection to a new and higher level of life. To "ascend" to a higher form of existence, a greater liberation, you must undergo a "descending" process, a dying to the elements in your total make-up that act as obstacles to a higher mode of existence. The more a person, on a purely secular level with no reflective reference to God, gives up his or her selfish aggrandizement by thinking of and helping others, the more he or she prepares for a fuller living according to the human nature God destined for him or her. The more you can do, by exercising your faith in God's loving and working presence in your life and through your work, to fashion the Body of Christ, by striving with greater purity of heart and fidelity to God's presences as outlined above, the more alive you will become. You will live out of God's love for love of God in God's love. You will surrender yourself to God's infinite power within you and within the moment, and experience freeing love in every action you perform in such awareness of your union with Him in work.

You humbly offer yourself and your gifts to God that, like Mary, the Mother of God, you may allow God to have His Word done in your work. God is calling you to share (*synergy*) in a working-with-God's creative power to use your gifts and talents to transfigure this universe into the Cosmic Christ. Rather than running away from involvement in the activities of this world, you move into the world, according to your talents and state of life, with enthusiasm and hope. What you add to make this world a better world in Christ, be it on a social, scientific, artistic, religious or whatever level, you believe will have an eternal effect on the whole process.

It is not enough to do your work out of a vague intention to form somehow or other the Body of Christ. You must first experience the *symbiosis* or the life with the Trinity within yourself. Touching God immanently present as energizing love within yourself in deep prayer each day, you will be driven by the indwelling Spirit of Jesus to desire to possess Him and to be possessed by Him. In your daily work, therefore, the creative presence of Christ is to be discovered by you in everyone and everything everywhere in a cosmic *diaphany* or a shining through of God's hidden features that become explicitly the outline of Christ in His Body according to Whom you and I have been created.

You learn to experience that everything becomes physically and literally lovable in God. You discover how God can be possessed and loved by you in everything around you. You no longer make an act of love while you are working. You now habitually love while you are working. Your work is your love. You are becoming love in every thought, word and deed. "Whatever you eat, whatever you drink, whatever you do at all, do it for the glory of God" (1 Cor 10:31).

Every breath you breathe is an act of love. You literally are praying all the time (1 Th 5:17), for you are seeking always to give God more glory and honor. He is becoming your God as you "excentrate" or move yourself away from yourself as your center of motivation, to "incentrate" or move yourself into the burning bush of God's presence within you and within each creature that you encounter.

THERE IS ONLY CHRIST

You live in the realization that Jesus Christ, the risen Lord, is the *Alpha*, the beginning, the image according to which not only you but the whole material world has been created. He is becoming for you at each moment as you live in Him, for and with Him, the *Omega*, the goal, the end toward which every finite creature is moving as toward a magnet that draws, by an active force of personal love, you and the entire universe.

In the person of Jesus Christ, vibrantly alive and inserted into your material world and working actively with your humble cooperation, is to be found the key to your sanctity and that is tied to loving service to bring about the fullness of meaning of the entire created cosmos. All has been created, including yourself, to be brought into the glorification of God. Jesus Christ is *now* accomplishing in the created universe the completion and fulfillment which His first coming began, a new creation, and which His second coming in the *Parousia* will reveal as the full manifestation of the total Christ: the risen Jesus as Head and you and I and the entire universe as parts united in the Body of Christ. This is the final, breath-taking vision that St. Paul gives to you, that is becoming realized in your doing all things in love:

> After that will come the end, when he hands over the kingdom to God the Father, having done away with every sovereignty, authority and power. For he must be king until he has put all his enemies under his feet and the last of the enemies to be destroyed is death, for everything is to be put under his feet. Though when it is said that everything is subjected, this clearly cannot include the One who subjected everything to him. And when everything is subjected to him, then the Son himself will be subject in his turn to the One who subjected all things to him, so that God may be all in all (1 Cor 15:24-28).

Chapter Thirteen

Intimate Presence to the Thou

In his play, *The Cocktail Party*, T.S. Eliot has powerfully satirized our modern, capitalistic society that has made of us human beings colonies of impersonalized ants, very efficiently running our colonies, but knowing no true human communication, knowing little of true love.

Celia, the Christ-image of the play, describes in the first act at a cocktail party how modern men and women are unable to communicate with each other:

> Everyone's alone—or so it seems to me. They make noises and think they are talking to each other. They make faces and think they understand each other. And I'm sure they don't.

At the end of the play, two years later, at a similar cocktail party, it is learned that Celia, who had become a Catholic nun and missionary, had been killed while tending the sick during a native uprising, apparently crucified, very near an ant hill. Her Christlike love for the natives, even to the point of dying for them, produces a tonic effect on those at the party. They seem able, in the light of her heroic love, to open up to each other better than before.

God has made us to live, not only in intimate oneness with Him sharing His life, but also in intimate love with others, especially in small communities of two, three, four, ten persons with whom we can share ourselves in the fellowship of the Spirit of love. There can be no true human happiness without love, for it is love that gives us identity and purpose in life. God has made us to love and to be loved. "It is not good that man should be alone. I will make him a helpmate" (Gn 2:18).

We have seen that God communicates something of Himself to us through His Word operating within all His creatures given to us as gifts of His love. He gives Himself directly through His Word, the Risen Jesus Christ, who lives within us and communes with us by leading us into the intimacy of His love for His Father through His Spirit of love. Yet God shares Himself with us in a creative experience of His love through the special gifts of human beings who love us deeply and whom we are privileged to love in the same reciprocal way. God's uncreated energies of love are experienced most when we, in unselfish giving and receiving love, meet His loving presence in others.

When we love another with deep intimacy and commitment, God is again made flesh in that love. "No one has ever seen God; but as long as we love one another God will live in us and his love will be complete in us" (1 Jn 4:12). We are called to be open and available to all human beings, made by our one Father to be our brothers and sisters, members of the Body of Christ, and united into a oneness through the Spirit of love.

But our human experiences demonstrate very evidently that, although our experience of God's abundant love drives us out to be "present" and available in love to all persons whom we meet, yet we lack the psychic power, the time and possibility of becoming intimate with masses of people. We need primal communities, bases of loving identity to which we go as to a "home" to become recreated and from which we go out to love others, but in a lesser intimacy.

AN *I-THOU* COMMUNITY

We stalk this earth in search of such a loving community

where we feel a return to the Garden of Eden. A harmony is developed with our own being of our body, soul and spirit powers as we enter into an on-going harmony and unity with the other. No longer is the other a person "over there" as an object. Love has broken down the barriers and in "ecstasy", or a standing out of our habitual control, we surrender to live for the happiness of the other. Now we know that our *I-ness* cannot be realized except in our "birthing" the other into his or her *Thou-ness*. In such deep, human love, transcendence and immanence merge into an *I-Thou* who become a *We* community.

When two persons are rooted in God and seek Him above all else, there is a basis for infinite richness. They both seek to surrender themselves to God for they know that only God's Spirit can teach them how to love each other in God's love and with His emptying power. They learn in their mutual love to find God. Each encounter is like a new discovery of God, loving and revealing Himself through their love. They can say to each other the beautiful words of St. John:

> Let us love one another
> since love comes from God
> and everyone who loves
> is begotten by God
> and knows God (1 Jn 4:7).

DANGERS AND FEARS

To the degree that one is gifted with a talent of great worth, to that degree such a talent may be abused. How often we have entered into a deep friendship and we were plagued with fears. As we learn in union with God to take the risk to open to such a person, we experience fears and doubts. Which way, Lord? How? What to do and how to say it? Above all, we find a true confrontation with our unredeemed, hidden areas that come out as we see ourselves being mirrored in the openness of the other. In such a loving friendship we begin to let down our defenses, as does the beloved. We listen to the depths of our inner self with all of its beauty unrealized before and also with all its demonic darkness.

Demands of sensitivity and fidelity not known before are made in proportion as we receive the gift of the other. Your *self* can no longer be the center of your value system as you are called humbly to serve only the unique godliness and happiness in the other. You could hesitate in such a call to intimacy. The demands might be too great, the sacrifices to self-centeredness too many. You might want to dash back quickly before it is too late to the flesh pots of Egypt away from the dark desert of living in deeper faith, hope and love.

What agony to let go and not hold on to the other! You experience a bit of Heaven in the oneness attained with the beloved. Whenever you have to leave such a deep sharing in oneness with the other, it is like cleaving yourself into two parts. You want more of what makes you happy. You are faced with the struggle: is it your happiness or the happiness of the other that is primary? In love you are gifted to love the other somewhat as God does, in a beautiful hope of what is yet unseen but could be. The one loved has not yet experienced himself or herself as good, noble or beautiful, yet in your eyes he or she is already truly lovable.

Yet in selfishness you can lose this sense of wonder and mystery, poetry and going beyond, and settle for impatiently demanding that the other person be more as you would wish or be more ready to satisfy your needs. You can fail to give yourself to God in His gift as that gift is presented in all of its beauty as well as in all your potential and actual imperfections. Patience is the love of God operating in us to give us hope that out of such imperfections something very beautiful can result. But this means a constant dying to your own aggressive moods to enter deeply into a oneness with God and the beloved so that the very human imperfections in you and the other can be sublimated and transformed by God's power of love in both of you. God's love becomes most realized in the patient struggle with trials and temptations toward selfishness or toward truly godly self-giving.

CHRISTIAN MARRIAGE

If you and I can experience the indwelling Trinity as loving us into new levels of being in the experience of a deep, intimate friendship, how much more should this type of intimate availability be found in marriage? Marriage is the most commonly experienced model of total availability in complete intimacy on body, soul and spiritual levels. All other intimate, one-to-one level relationships are built upon the model of marriage. We all come from a father and mother. We grew up and shared in their intimacy toward each other. We are the results now of their shared love and thus we can experience God in our human love relationships, even if we are not in a marriage relationship, to the degree that such intimacy has come to us through parents and married friends who share their love with us as a fruit of their mutual self-giving. Such married persons have a special call to show celibate and single persons how to live in deep intimacy and how to experience God in that very self-giving to another, as a fruit of their intimacy with each other which they share with others in their outreach in parish, social and work relationships.

That two persons can truly live constantly, however, in the among Christians marriage is considered a sacrament, a mysterious action of Jesus Christ extended through His Church whereby two persons wedded to each other can share

His glorious life within the Trinity living in the husband and wife. In marriage, Jesus gives His Spirit of love to these two persons. They can share in their self-giving to each other the very self-giving of God to each other and to both of them as a one in Christ.

This Christian sublime ideal is described by St. Paul as a great mystery:

> Give way to one another in obedience to Christ. Wives should regard their husbands as they regard the Lord, since as Christ is head of the Church and saves the whole body, so is a husband the head of his wife; and as the Church submits to Christ, so should wives to their husbands, in everything. Husbands should love their wives just as Christ loved the Church and sacrificed himself for her to make her holy. . . . In the same way, husbands must love their wives as they love their own bodies; for a man to love his wife is for him to love himself. A man never hates his own body, but he feeds it and looks after it; and that is the way Christ treats the Church, because it is his body and we are its living parts. For this reason, a man must leave his father and mother and be joined to his wife, and the two will become one body. This mystery has many implications; but I am saying it applies to Christ and the Church. . . . To sum up, you too, each one of you, must love his wife as he loves himself; and let every wife respect her husband (Ep 5:21-33).

TRANSFORMING POWER OF CONJUGAL LOVE

The most powerful image of God's total self-giving to human beings is found ideally in marriage as man and woman as whole persons, made of "ensouled" bodies and "embodied" souls, seek to incarnate their interior love in a physical material expression. Yet so many marriages, especially among Christians, do not become the community of ecstatic, self-giving in passionate desire for the other as it should be in a continued growth, primarily because of a faulty dualism inherited from Platonism through Augustinianism and Jansenism that all too often considered matter and hence sex as evil. We need to understand body, soul and spirit, not as parts that can be independent of each other, but as levels of manifesting the inner person in all his or her striving toward loving union with another. The primal symbol of sexual intercourse completes the spiritual intimacy found within each partner as God's own activity in His self-giving to the two members of the marriage. The human body is not an instrument that "makes love", but it is the whole person seeking to attain union through self-sacrificing love that goes out and becomes one with the other as the two enter into each other in ecstasy. The two become one body.

The ecstasy of oneness attained is an experience of total oneness in a body, soul, spirit intercourse. So great and complete is the intended giving of oneself to the other that is posited by the primal symbol of intercourse, that such a union cries out for a stable monogamous commitment to each other. Such a oneness begs for a continued self-giving and receiving the unique gift of the other in all phases of human living, not only in the act of conjugal self-giving but concretely in washing the dishes, going to monotonous work, caring for the children: sharing, in a word, all facets of human living, since the two are one and yet want to become still more and more one in the sharing of all life's activities.

To posit such a symbol of total self-giving with many others promiscuously is to act out a lie of a loving, self-sacrificing act without carrying through with a permanent commitment. And yet such a true love for the other will allow "space" that the other may develop in new and different ways that the first member may not appreciate. Each member must be allowed freedom to have his or her own friends and interests. The poet, Kahlil Gibran, warns against an all too possessing spirit:

> Give your hearts, but not into each
> other's keeping.
> For only the hand of life can contain
> your hearts.
> And stand together yet not too near
> together:
> For the pillars of the temple stand apart,
> and the oak tree and the cypress grow
> not in each other's shadow (*The Prophet*, pp. 15-16).

OPENNESS TO A THIRD PERSON

We have spoken about the source of all reality as the Trinity, an *I-Thou* in a *We*-community. If marriage is the most primal and powerful experience of God as self-giving and indwelling of a community of an *I-Thou* relationship, it too leads such shared love into a begetting of a third. The love of the two in marriage converges in the single flame of love that brings forth a third. Such conjugal love, as the Church has always taught, is always open to this third, a new begetting, an enfleshing of such love in a new life.

Directly the ecstatic love of the husband and wife wants to incarnate their mutual love in a new person who concretely and for all eternity will express that ecstatic oneness attained. The begetting and bringing into the fullness of this new life will deepen in another concrete expression of self-giving between husband and wife. Indirectly they wish to give their on-going, growing oneness of love that they have mutually experienced, to their children that they may have begotten. But the giving to the "third" does not stop within the family circle. Their begetting, by their mutual love, of others into new life of love and self-identity extends to others outside the family and immediate blood-line, to other persons whom the husband and wife are privileged to serve. When new children cannot be begotten as an expression of loving oneness, an outlet is found in building other We-communities that extend the *I-Thou* into new *We*-communities beyond the family.

CONTEMPLATION IN MARRIAGE

God's most intimate presence as self-giving is experienced when two abide in love. They then abide in God and God abides in them, as it is said in 1 Jn 4:16. Conjugal oneness calls out a mutual stretching in transcendence continuously to go beyond the level of oneness attained. For any union attained dies unless it is rooted in a stretching, in the ecstasy of passionate desire to give oneself more and more to the beloved. As husband and wife experience in the faith, hope and love shown toward each other in intimate union a oneness also with God, who by His uncreated energies of love is experienced as the source of the gift of love, so they stretch out to find God within their abiding love.

At the same time that they "contemplate" their oneness in the uniqueness of the other with a burning desire to live in loving service to fulfill the other in happiness, they experience God as their ultimate source of union and happiness. They are moved to live in loving service to Him.

DANGERS IN MARRIAGE

Many dangers to an on-going growth in self-giving to the other in marriage stem from our affluent society, filled with so many material riches that tend toward self-centeredness and not to unselfish sacrifice for others. Love in such a modern context can so often be eroticism and not true *agape*, self-giving. Married people can so easily exploit the other as an object or a "thing" to be possessed and used in a sensuous self-seeking. Such intimacy, as marriage opens each partner to share, opens them also to the unredeemed, hidden areas that come out as they see themselves being mirrored in the openness of the other. Unless two persons in marriage are moving in the Spirit of Jesus, they can so easily lose the contemplative spirit of wonder and mystery and settle for getting "something" from each other in terms of orgasmic pleasures.

A constant state of vigilance is necessary to avoid selfish "possession" of the other and to live in a spirit of trust toward the other. Suspicions about the other must be replaced by genuine openness to share any fears and doubts and frustrations even with the other. To do this, there is a need for individual prayer to encounter the indwelling power of the Trinity who alone can make all things possible. Communal sharing in the presence of God is also a great help toward openness to the transcendence in each other. The sacraments of the Rite of Reconciliation and the Eucharist are powerful means of purifying the heart and healing the brokenness that married life so easily reveals when two persons are honestly searching for God's inner strength.

A TRANSFIGURATION

Marriage is a microcosm of society and the entire universe that is destined to become one in the Body of Christ. As the two spouses open themselves to God's personalized energies of love in their love, they have strength to believe in the transfigurating power of God who wishes to accomplish the same unification in the entire world. Out of their own brokenness they experience a transfiguration into Christ. To that degree, they can move into a broken world to cooperate with Christ to transform it by their loving service.

No one is ever called merely to experience the indwelling

presence of God. Nor are we called into an intimate friendship to stay there in a selfish "a deux" that replaces or rather heightens the selfishness of an isolated person. Nor are married persons called into a oneness with each other to build up walls against a broken world and to enjoy unending happiness within the protective walls of "splendid isolation." The transformation that they progressively experience allows them to hope that with the power of the risen Jesus, the Divine Physician, they can transcend the brokenness and meaninglessness of the human situations surrounding them by bringing their love with the love of God to others.

Unsuspected energies are released in the discovery of God's transforming power in their mutual love. These energies of love pour out into the tasks of everyday living. They cooperate humbly and generously with God's immanent, loving presence in each event of life. They accept the challenge to become reconcilers of the world to God (2 Cor 5:17-20). A new-founded openness to care for others in loving service becomes a daily experience on a global level, but above all, concretely in the immediate human relationships that surround them.

A LOVING CHURCH

Love begets love and the living members, two cells that are healthily in love with each other and build each other up by God's love within them, begin to touch other members to call them into new life. Spouses in their social relationships to others contemplate the same process experienced in their conjugal oneness and strive to cooperate with the Spirit to build up the Body of Christ into new richness, a new unity in diversity where, in the words of Teilhard de Chardin, "Love differentiates as it unites."

They use their gifts and charisms in loving service as they "inscape" into the material world and there become co-creators of new life in the material world.

To be vibrant members of the Body of Christ, the Church, they have need for intimate moments to be alone with God and also to be together in deep oneness with the Trinity. The community that they experience in their love of a trinitarian God, Father, Son and Holy Spirit, will become their strength as they seek prayerfully to build similar communities rooted in God's oneness in diversity.

They will understand that true union with God and true contemplation are measured by love for others in humble service. Authentic holiness is living out in each human relationship, not only those in marriage, the Christian Baptism of death to selfishness and a rising with the Spirit of the risen Jesus to live for others. Such sanctity unfolds in the monotony of daily life-situations. Marriage is a privilege in which two persons progressively learn to fall in love with each other and with God simultaneously. It becomes for married persons the basic experience allowing for loving service to project outward into a series of unending, loving communities.

This is the end of God's creative order, the fulfillment of Jesus' constant prayer to the Father:

> May they all be one.
> Father, may they be one in us,
> as you are in me and I am in you,
> so that the world may believe it was you who sent me.
> I have given them the glory you gave to me,
> that they may be one as we are one.
> With me in them and you in me,
> may they be so completely one
> that the world will realize that it was you who sent me

and that I have loved them as much as you loved me. . . .
I have made your name known to them
and will continue to make it known,
so that the love with which you loved me may be in them,
and so that I may be in them (Jn 17:21-26).

Chapter Fourteen

Loving All Beings In Christ

In his most provocative novel, *Silence*, Japanese novelist and Catholic convert, Shusaku Endo, shocks us out of our habitual way of conceiving the love of God and the love of neighbor. Fr. Sebastian Rodriguez, a Portuguese Jesuit, goes to Japan in order to find his former beloved teacher, Fr. Ferreria. The latter, it was rumored, had apostatized in order to avoid martyrdom. After much underground missionary activity helping the small remnant of Christians, the young priest is captured and put into prison.

Fr. Ferreria is sent to him to tell him why he really apostatized in the hopes of convincing Fr. Sebastian to do likewise. The old priest had to watch with horror as his Christian faithful were subject to the agonizing tortures of a slow death. He was told that if he trampled on the bronze image of Christ and His Mother he could stop the sufferings of the other Christian prisoners.

"The reason, are you ready?" says Ferreria, "Listen, I was put in here and heard the voices of those people for whom God did nothing. God did not do a single thing. I prayed with all my strength but God did nothing. . . . Certainly Christ would have apostatized for them" (pp. 253-256). The young priest has the same experience of a suffering Christ who would sacrifice everything in order to save His people from suffering.

"And then the Christ in bronze speaks to the priest:

'Trample, trample! I more than anyone know of the pain in your foot. Trample! It was to be trampled on by men that I was born into this world. It was to share men's pain that I carried My cross' " (p. 259). The two priests had discovered the silence of the God they had known in their habitual way of worshiping Him in the security of an intellectual religion with its assuring doctrines and rituals. But they discovered the God of pain, of an emptying and stripped God in Christ who is ready to enter into ignominy and humiliation before the world of their Christianity to spare their fellow Christians from further suffering.

FORSAKEN LOVE

This example highlights the essence of true love that is ready to be emptied of everything in order to give all out of love for others. It is a readiness to be cast down into the abyss as Jesus experienced on the cross, where the individual Christian is tossed about in all directions, in a kind of darkness where there is no distinction between up and down, the "right" and the "wrong" way of doing things: the readiness to undergo an abandonment by the Heavenly Father and to be delivered into the hands of Satan, the great tempter, who can taunt him with final perdition. Yet love for the neighbor will be the only anchor-hold with which to confront the awesome, uncontrollable God.

This is the love that Jesus has shown us in His agony and death on the cross. Yet He was only imaging the love that the Father has for Him and for all of us in Him. "As the Father has loved me, so I have loved you" (Jn 15:9). He promises us simply that if we should obey His commands and live in His love by loving others with a similar love that is a continued readiness to lay down one's life for a friend, the Father and He would "come to him and make our home with him" (Jn 14:23). That very love of God is within the baptized Christian, empow-

ering him to love with God's very own love. What you cannot
do by your own power you can do by God's uncreated energies
of love living within you.

You have received from the Holy Spirit a powerful infusion to be able to live within that loving trinitarian family. The
more you experience God's self-giving in the intimate loving
relationships of Father, Son and Holy Spirit, the more you can
go out and love others in that very indwelling love of the
Trinity. ". . . as long as we love one another God will live in us
and his love will be complete in us . . . and anyone who lives in
love lives in God and God lives in him" (1 Jn 4:12, 16).

And the reason becomes clearer each day as you strive to
put on the mind of Christ. St. Paul gives you that reason: "And
this is because the love of Christ overwhelms us when we
reflect that if one man has died for all, then all men should be
dead; and the reason he died for all was so that living men
should live no longer for themselves, but for him who died and
was raised to life for them" (2 Cor 5:14-15). You can go forth,
not only in the intimacy of a loving community of an *I-Thou*
with God or with chosen friends, but in the world of strangers,
other human beings, who have not given you their love in any
depth, and there you can bring forth the love-power of God
Himself in their lives. For you live no longer you yourself but
Christ Jesus lives within you (Gal 2:20).

ONE COMMANDMENT

You have been seized by Christ and His love urges you
outward to the world community made up of so many diverse
human beings in whom is stamped the image and likeness of
Christ. As you yield yourself to the transforming power of the
Spirit of Jesus living within you, you realize that you cannot
love God without loving your neighbor, for love of God unites
you with His power and drives you forth to love all beings

6

uniquely created by God's love to share His intimate life.

With St. Paul you burn with love for Christ. You seek only Him and consider all other things as worthless and as dung, but to possess Him and live out of love for Him who has loved you so infinitely. As you surrender to the Hound of Heaven who had chased you down the arches of the years and down the labyrinthine ways of your own mind and in the midst of tears, as Francis Thompson describes it (*The Hound of Heaven*), so you too join the Good Shepherd in the pursuit of others who have not yet surrendered to "love's uplifted stroke."

You know the great joy of living in Christ and the Father's Spirit of love. You burn to sacrifice yourself to bring others to Christ. You are ready to do all to alleviate all sufferings, physical, psychic or spiritual in the lives of your neighbors, whoever or wherever they may be. You are ready to give to the hungry and thirsty; to clothe the naked and visit and comfort the sick and those in prison because it is the love of Christ within you that seeks to incarnate itself in others through your caring love (Mt 25:35-36).

> So though I am not a slave of any man I have made myself the slave of everyone so as to win as many as I could. I made myself a Jew to the Jews, to win the Jews; that is, I who am not a subject of the Law made myself a subject of the Law to those who are the subjects of the Law, to win those who are subject to the Law . . . . For the weak I made myself weak. I made myself all things to all men in order to save some at any cost; and I still do this, for the sake of the gospel, to have a share in its blessings (1 Cor 9:19-23).

ONENESS WITH ALL BEINGS

The power of love is to unite what has been separated or divided. It brings into harmony and unity a diversity, without destroying the differences but rather exalting them into their very uniqueness so that the love of God is glorified in such individuated love for each of His creatures. The more you are raised by God's Spirit to the intimate presence of God, Father, Son and Spirit, living and loving within you with an infinite love, the more you begin to enter into communion, a union with other human beings and also all other sub-human creatures. There develops within you a genuine sense of being one with the whole world, of being open and ready to give yourself to the world in loving service to draw out the happiness and well-being of each creature. Strangely, the paradox of love is that the more you lose-yourself for love of others in service to them, the more you find your true self in the oneness you share with them in Christ.

This oneness that you begin to experience as you turn toward others in need of healing love, can never be out of a sense of condescending compassion and pity that denigrates the inner beauty locked within each person and creature that you encounter. As you discover God within His creatures, you discover the most intimate bond of all creation as held in God's uncreated energies of love permeating all things. You surrender to serve that divine love. The true test of your authentic love for God will always be the degree of self-giving of yourself to other human beings.

There can be in the prayer-life of an individual a period of being ill at ease with a going-out toward others. You may at first want to retire and immerse all of your attention upon the indwelling Trinity. How sweet is such a communion! And how alarming is the brokenness and imperfections of other human beings who make demands on your time and patience! As you fix your attention upon the indwelling presence of God, you feel that all human involvement seems useless and banal. This can be a source of humiliation as you feel your impotence to give yourself sufficiently to the needs of others, especially those closest to you in your immediate community. Even when you wish to serve others, at times you lack the know-how to effect in human terms a going out and a giving of yourself in concrete loving service. We do need experience in bringing the inner desire of wanting to serve others to actuality and that means learning how to break sometimes our basic tendencies that may be more introspective, to become more outgoing in the service and ministry to others. As long as you keep this humble desire to be open and self-giving to all who come into your life and never close yourself off in self-centeredness, God's Spirit will be operating and opening up avenues to you of greater self-giving.

QUALITIES OF TRUE LOVE

As you yield yourself more completely each day to the transforming power of the Spirit of the risen Lord, living within you, you begin to test your loving service by the characteristics given by St. Paul of true love. You soon realize the difference between the standard of the world as to what is great and important, and God's standard of true, loving service. You, with St. Paul, quickly enough realize that you may possess great gifts of understanding, prophecy, knowing all knowledge, possessing faith strong enough to move mountains, giving millions of dollars to the poor, even giving up your own body to be burned, but if you do not possess true self-sacrificing love all these talents and good works would only be a gong booming or a cymbal clashing. True love has the following characteristics:

> Love is always patient and kind. It is never jealous; love is never boastful or conceited; it is never rude or selfish; it does not take offence, and is not resentful. Love takes no pleasure in other people's sins but delights in the truth; it is always ready to

excuse, to trust, to hope, and to endure whatever comes. Love does not come to an end (1 Cor 13:4-8).

In each of your encounters with other human persons, you seek to live this kind of love. You praise God for the successes in others. You see the goodness in each person. You hope in that goodness and labor to bring it forth, as St. Paul wanted to be the mid-wife to bring his faithful into a new life in Christ. You seek to sublimate your petty, "carnal" feelings of hurt pride, envy, jealousy, anger by bringing them under the healing power of Jesus Christ living in you and in the other. Humility is the index of your proper love for yourself that allows you to give yourself in honesty as a gift to others.

Is this not the end of our lives, to experience in the core of our beings the Trinity, living and loving and transforming us individually into beautiful people, children of God, who then can give away that beauty and call out new beauty in others by the gift of ourselves to them?

More consciously you wish to do everything under the loving power of Jesus Christ. You yield your whole being to His direction. His love you allow to flow out through your eyes, your touch, your loving embrace as you become Christ's love to others. In your conscious union with Christ who permeates every part of your being with His risen life, you offer yourself to serve His majesty. St. Symeon the New Theologian (†1022) describes this conscious union that you gradually can attain:

> We become members of Christ—and Christ
> becomes our members,
> Christ becomes my hand, Christ, my miserable foot;
> and I, unhappy one, am Christ's hand, Christ's foot!
> I move my hand, and my hand is the whole Christ
> since, do not forget it, God is indivisible in His divinity—;
> I move my foot, and behold it shines like That—one!
> Do not accuse me of blasphemy, but welcome these things

and adore Christ who makes you such,
since if you so wish you will become a member of Christ,
and similarly all our members individually
will become members of Christ and Christ our members,
all which is dishonorable in us He will make honorable
by adorning it with His divine beauty and His divine glory,
since living with God at the same time, we shall become gods,
no longer seeing the shamefulness of our body at all,
but made completely like Christ in our whole body,
each member of our body will be the whole Christ;
because, becoming many members, He remains unique and
indivisible, and each part is He, the whole Christ. . . .
It is truly a marriage which takes place, ineffable and divine:
God unites Himself with each one—yes, I repeat it,
it is my delight—and each becomes one with the Master
(Hymn 15).

HUMILITY

If the Holy Spirit of the indwelling Trinity is leading you
in true love in all of your human relationships with other
persons, you will know surely when you are moving in true love
by the humility you manifest in your human relationships. The
Spirit of authentic love brings you into an inner freedom
because you are experiencing from within your inner beauty in
God's infinite love for you. In that freedom that admits of
great growth you find yourself giving up your aggressive attacks upon others and upon the nature of God around you. A
gentleness of spirit pervades your entire being on all levels,
body, soul and spirit. A deeper receptivity than that which you
formerly manifested allows you to encounter more of God in
the other person.

Such humility is able to transform pride and self-
containment and express in your looks, words and actions that

you sincerely stand in need of others to love and serve. Your *being* depends upon them. You cannot be who you are unless you move toward them in loving self-giving.

Such total availability opens yourself to being refused, rejected and wounded by others. But because the presence of God's Spirit of love is so strongly operating in you, you can surrender such hurts so that greater love may come forth. You can truly learn in your loving service toward others to turn the other cheek and go that extra mile. You learn to avoid turning away into isolation at the first sign of rejected love. You put on the magnanimity of Jesus, the image of the Father, as He forgives others who rejected His perfect and complete love for them. You transcend the pain and hurt by experiencing in deep hope that presence of God, loving both you and the others, and calling all into a greater union with Him and with each other.

GOD EVERYWHERE

Not only does the experience of God dwelling within you increase your awareness of God dwelling and operating to bring you and other human beings into a greater oneness in His Son, but it increases your oneness with all God's creatures. A global sense of God's presence comes over you in your encounter with even the sub-human cosmos, the entire material creation of God. You are given new eyes of faith, hope and love to see God's grandeur bursting forth as Gerard Manley Hopkins expressed it in his poem, *God's Grandeur*: "The world is charged with the grandeur of God. It will flame out, like shining from shook foil."

A grain of wheat, the sunset in the west bursting through splintering clouds with its ball of fire, the innocent smile of a baby, the wisdom of an old man sharing his experiences of the godly in his life on a park bench; all things cry out to you that

God is here, this place is indeed holy! You take off your shoes
of securities and approach with awe and reverence. No longer
is the world "secular" but it is bombarded in all its materiality
with the Spirit of God's love.

Hopkins once wrote a beautiful description of God's uncreated energies of love invading all of God's material universe. "All things are charged with love, are charged with God
and if we know how to touch them, give off sparks and take
fire, yield drops and flow, ring and tell of him." With eyes of a
child filled with wonder and poetry, you open to God's living
revelation in all things. You believe that nothing can keep out
the loving, inside presence of God as love in all things. As you
act on that living faith, it becomes a reality. More and more,
every moment with all your material involvement allows you to
become more and more united with the inside, indwelling
presence of God, the triune community of *I-Thou* in a *We*, of
self-giving Persons.

A LOVING ENERGY IN THE WORLD

Heaven is not only contemplating your oneness with the
triune God. It is also giving yourself in greater love to serve
others. Contemplation is not to be a static gazing upon the
beauties of this world, but it begins with experiencing God's
presence as you actively surrender yourself to be His energizing love toward all human persons whom you meet and toward
all animals, plants and inanimate creatures. It is only in your
active receptivity of God's energies of love operating within
each of His creatures, that God's presence as loving energy can
be released within this world and be "reconciled through him
and for him" (Col 1:20).

The whole material world with each atom created by
God's loving energies becomes the "place" where you can
adore God and surrender to His loving presence as you seek to

serve Him in humble love by serving each creature. You praise God not only because of His gifts to you, but above all for His very own loving presence. The distinction between what is painful, a setback and humiliation, a calamity and what is pleasant, a success and honor, disappears as you see through all events and creatures that touch your life, and see all things as "signs" of God's great love for you and all mankind. "Be it done unto me, according to thy Word" becomes your constant, prayerful act of surrender.

Your awareness of God's presence as love penetrates every thought, word and deed. Nothing in the created order of material creatures prevents you from growing in greater love and purity of heart to see God ever more in every part of His created universe. You stretch out your empty hands and humbly ask God to fill them with His energies of love. You pray incessantly because at every moment your desire is that God be glorified. Surrender to God at each moment is the sign of true human freedom. The joy of entering into the conscious awareness of what you will experience for all eternity in the condition called Heaven is already yours as you live, not only as a child of your Heavenly Father, one with Christ His only begotten Son in His Spirit, but as you also live one with your brothers and sisters of the entire human race arfd one with every material, sub-human creature made by God for His glory.

You already are living in the Heavenly Jerusalem: "You see this city? Here God lives among men. He will make his home among them; they shall be his people, and he will be their God; his name is God-with-them. He will wipe away all tears from their eyes; there will be no more death, and no more mourning or sadness. The world of the past has gone" (Rv 21:3-4).

Chapter Fifteen

Releasing God's Presence in the World

You have surely experienced many times the movement from absence toward presence as you met a stranger on a plane, train or wherever providence brought you into the possibility of a further growth into your being, and allowed the stranger to discover in your openness his or her *being*. So often on your journey through life you are thrown next to people whom you have never met before. They sit close to you. They are "objects" next to you, "over there," until one smiles or says a kind word of interest to the other. The mystery of presence begins when one becomes "present" in his or her words and gestures that communicate the mysterious message that says: "I do not know you. We are closed to each. But I would like to be open for you. Let us be mutually available to the other."

Such a mystery of presence cannot be forced, nor can it be understood and willed for any pragmatic motive. It admits of various levels of becoming present to the other, as two people move away from the controlled object—object relationship into the movement of one toward the other as toward a possible other self. *Availability* is the act by which you incline yourself freely to be a presence to another.

Being a presence toward another admits of great intensity, depending on how unselfishly you wish to give yourself in loving service to the other in affective and effective love. Passing acquaintances usually do not develop into deep presences. For this, time and intimate sharing are necessary. Deep love presence between two persons is rooted in a desire to live for the other's complete good and happiness. You would do anything to bring to actuality the complete fulfillment of the other.

Such a love presence takes place secondly in a *mutuality*, in an *I-Thou* relationship as the two interchange the gift of each other. Such presence is intensified as you do not selfishly look for anything in return; yet there is a mutual gifting which becomes all the stronger when you forget about the returned gift and concentrate only on the gift of yourself.

Thirdly, presence demands an actualization of the exchange. Presence that is not experienced as self-gifting in a coming together, will become an absence if never renewed in giving. There is always a need for communion or sharing the oneness in spirit. Here presence increases as you empty all, both the good and even the weakness, in trusting, self-gifting revelation of yourself in the most intimate, deepest levels of sharing your total "person" with the other.

GOD'S PRESENCE TO US

We have been discussing in various ways that God is love by His nature and that therefore He is also "presence" as self-giving by His very nature. But in what way can you and I experience God's presence to us? How can we live to make God happy? How can God who is so completely perfect and immutable receive anything from us that would add anything to His personhood? Does God really wish to share His being with us to the degree of "communion," where we truly can become one with Him? We have touched here and there in the previous chapters on the qualities of God's presence to us. We have seen how God's Word became flesh and dwelt among us in the person of Jesus Christ to invite us to receive the gift of God's very being in the most intimate friendship. "Yes, God loved the world so much that he gave his only Son, so that everyone who believes in him may not be lost but may have eternal life" (Jn 3:16). God establishes in Jesus Christ, through His death and resurrection, the New Covenant whereby God pledges to commit Himself not only to share with us His gifts for our happiness, but to commit Himself in the gift of Himself to us unto our total happiness. ". . . . but he (God) does it all for our own good, so that we may share his own holiness" (Heb 12:10).

God pours into our hearts His love through the Spirit whom He gives us (Rm 5:5) and who dwells within us (Rm 8:9), in order that in His Spirit we might know that we are really children of God (1 Jn 3:1), made heirs with Christ of Heaven forever (Rm 8:17). Jesus is the way, the truth and the life who leads us into the most intimate presence of the Trinity which wishes effectively to come and abide within us, Father, Son and Spirit (Jn 14:23).

If God wishes for us a presence of availability unto our complete happiness in our awareness of our eternal sonship and daughtership within His family, we too can live unto God's happiness, glory and praise. We praise God most when we live consciously in Christ in order that with His mind we may glorify the Father in His Spirit of love.

We can also enter into a mutual sharing with God. God lives within us and raises us up by His free gift of Himself in His uncreated energies of love that are grace, divinizing us into participators of His very own nature (2 P 1:4). By God's gratuitous self-gift we are made worthy to receive His fullness of presence, His availability toward us unto our complete happiness, but we too can share ourselves with God when at every moment we seek with Jesus to do God's holy will. Jesus had this for his mutual self-gift back to the Father from whom He received the gift of the Father. " . . . because my aim is to do not my own will, but the will of him who sent me" (Jn 5:30).

Such a desire to share ourselves with God who shares Himself, Father, Son and Holy Spirit, so perfectly and completely, promotes us to seek at all times to live in greater awareness of our communication with God as He gives us His Word. How we ought to burn with desire never to lose this consciousness of being one with God, communing at each moment in the events of our lives with God as our Ultimate Source and End of our very being! We wish to live in love more consciously as we are aware of our oneness in God's communicating Love. We are ready to put to death everything that impedes the new life lived in communion with the Trinity. "Every thought is our prisoner, captured to be brought into obedience to Christ. Once you have given your complete obedience, we are prepared to punish any disobedience" (2 Cor 10:5-6).

RELEASING GOD'S PRESENCE IN THE WORLD

You have moved from being closed to being open to God, and you become intensely aware of God communing with you at all times with His infinite love within you. You wish at all times to pray as you seek in all things to love God with your whole heart and with all your strength (Dt 6:5). You are also driven outward toward the world in which you live. You wish to share your new-founded *being*, discovered in God's great love for you. It is always a movement, therefore, outward toward those human beings around you that you go to become God's presence of love toward all whom you are privileged to meet and to whom you become available to call them into their being through the mystery of your unique presence.

God's presence is infinite; His love is total and complete. Yet the experience of God's presence is quite dependent on you and me releasing His love in the context of our human situation. God calls others into being by the love of God in us, shown in genuine, loving presence to those others. I experienced this call into presence the other day, that is always a *becoming*, an unending series of being birthed into new being. After concelebrating a beautiful Liturgy, I overheard one of the concelebrating priests turn to one of the little acolytes to ask his name. "John, it was a real privilege to be on the altar today with you," the priest told the boy with great sincerity. It was a genuine openness to the *I* in that young boy. The priest was God's presence to him in that moment, as the boy understood that he was important in the eyes of that priest. That boy could better understand now that he was also beautiful in the eyes of God Himself.

TENSIONED LIVING

Yet why are you and I not capable of being God's presence to others at all times? One difficulty lies in the tension between the inner, living experience of the indwelling Trinity, and the outward giving of that love and new life to others. It is a tension between the eternal *now* experienced in those moments of aloneness with the *Alone*, and this present temporal *now* that is so full of absence of love and openness in self-giving to others. There is a tension and brokenness that more easily separates contemplation from daily living, than it unites into the same presence of love for God and neighbor.

We Christians have responded in several ways to God's presence within us and beyond us in the world around us. Through an excessive objectivizing form of Christian spirituality we modern Christians live in two worlds that in reality, in God's real presence, are not two separated worlds: the world of matter and the world of spirit. We are drawn by the beauties of this world and the challenge to make it an ever more beautiful place in which to live. Yet our Christian *credo* tells us on the other hand that these ephemeral material things will soon pass

away and that we must lift our hearts and our eyes heaven-
ward. Heaven awaits us if we do not take too seriously this
present form of existence. One cannot after all love both God
and mammon at the same time. Thus we feel a dull pull: one
drawing us to full citizenship in this earthly city; the other
recalling our future citizenship in the City of Heaven that gives
us eternity over this temporal existence.

We can face this dilemma and answer it firstly by ignoring
and repressing the desires for the things of the created world,
and live for "the things above" through a philosophy of flight
from the present world. Other people will be looked upon as
"instruments" or occasions whereby we can do good to gain
Heaven. We will fail to open ourselves to an immediate experience of the unique divine indwelling in that person. In such a
view there will be no true presence to other human beings, nor
will there be any true presence to God.

We can answer this tension secondly by turning away from
the other-worldly values and living completely in and for this
world, without any openness to the transcendent God who
alone must be served. Our openness to others on the horizon-
tal plane soon closes into a selfish pragmatism of doing good to
be known as a "do-gooder."

Thirdly we can respond to this necessary tension by mak-
ing a compromise that results in a split personality which
would now live for God, now for the world, with hardly a
synthesis or resolution of the dilemma. Perhaps most of us
Christians are in this category of spiritual "schizophrenics"
who never feel comfortable either with God or with neighbor,
with the spiritual order or the material existence.

Yet there is a true Christian synthesis that presents itself as
the fourth alternative. This consists in reconciling the tension
between a deep love of God and intimate sense of His abiding
presence within us, and a passionate love of the world where
we also find the same abiding presence of the all-loving God.

We can become intimately present to the things of this world to draw out the richness that God has implanted with His creatures, and yet live in a detachment from the things of this world that will free us to become even more present both to God and His creatures.

NOTHING IS PROFANE

For those who have the eyes to see, God is everywhere inserted into His material creation and working to bring it into its fulfillment unto His glory and the sharing of His own life and happiness with His human creatures. The divine presence through the physical, created world assails us, penetrates and moulds us. God shouts out from inside of each material moment in space and time that He is here present, and that this place is holy by His presence as an activating, loving energy. God is revealing Himself everywhere, through our groping efforts, as a universal milieu, an environment, the air that we breathe. All beings have full reality and are holy in proportion as they converge upon this Ultimate Point. God is the source of all perfections and the goal toward which created beings are moving in an *élan vital* to their completion.

This vision of worshipful communion between you and your Divine Creator, whereby you can lose yourself in God as in an "Other," is grounded in the Word Incarnate, Jesus Christ. In Him, as St. Paul teaches with such insistence, all things are reunited and are consummated. By the resurrectional presence of Christ who fills all things, the whole of creation has a meaningful consistency.

By your loving actions done in love of God and neighbor, no matter how insignificant the works may be, you are capable of releasing God's presence within the world by building up the Body of Christ until it will reach its consummation when Christ will appear in His fullness of glory at the end of time, and recapitulate under Himself as Head the whole created order.

A MERCIFUL GOD

We might confuse, however, our doing good deeds, even out of such a sublime motive as helping to build the Body of Christ, with true love. If God's very nature is to be love, we see in Scripture and in our own history of relationships between ourselves and God that God's presence as love is released and manifested in human history in His many acts of mercy.

Over and over in Scripture God's love is described as a forgiving, seeking, involving, sharing condescension, not merely as a merciful act but as a God who is *mercy*. "Yahweh is tender and compassionate, slow to anger, most loving. . . . No less than the height of heaven over earth is the greatness of his love for those who fear him; he takes our sins farther away than the east is from the west" (Ps 103:8, 11, 12). "Give thanks to Yahweh, for he is good, his love is everlasting!" (Ps. 106:1).

Abraham J. Heschel, the great Jewish theologian, describes God as a merciful, involving God: "He is the father of all men, not only a judge; he is a lover engaged to his people, not only a king. God stands in a passionate relationship to man. His love or anger, his mercy or disappointment is an expression of his profound participation in the history of Israel and all men" (*Man Is Not Alone*; p. 244).

But God's greatest mercy is shown when He sent into our world His Son, Jesus Christ. Here we see love as total self-giving. God in Jesus bends down into our misery and takes upon Himself our nature in order that God's presence as love may be most manifest.

> But God loved us with so much love that he was generous with his mercy: when we were dead through our sins, he brought us to live with Christ—it is through grace that you have been

saved. He raised us up with him and gave us a place with him in heaven, in Christ Jesus (Ep 2:4-6).

Grace in Scripture and in the writings of the early Eastern Fathers is not an "accident," a thing that God gives to us or does for us, but is primarily God in His uncreated energies of love giving Himself in a forgiving, seeking, sharing of His being with us, emptying Himself so that we might be filled with His goodness, with His very own being.

BLESSED ARE THE MERCIFUL

When Jesus preached His beatitudes He announced the Kingdom of God, a sharing in the very family of God, to be given to those who were poor in spirit and who showed mercy to each other. Many wanted God's individual acts of mercy but as a relief from their misery and oppression by foreign rulers, and as the acquisition of the wealth of this earth. They were not listening to His message that He was the incarnation of God's mercy as the active presence of God's love come among them, if they would only surrender their lives to Him and in His Spirit would live in love. He was saying that in Him they would find strength to become merciful love to others, because they would be releasing by their goodness and merciful love to others the goodness and mercy of God Himself. Not by doing merciful deeds by our own power, but by doing it in His experienced presence as merciful love to us would we discover what was always there: God is merciful love and gives Himself beyond all His other gifts to all who open up to receive God Himself as His greatest gift.

You are not to show mercy in your human existence to others and then God will begin to show mercy to you. But when you show compassionate love and mercy to others, then God's merciful love will become manifested. God is by nature always loving and therefore always merciful in His condescending energies of love for self-giving. When you are merciful, you unleash God's infinite mercy. God's mercy becomes incarnate and in the world around you, you can see and know that God is an involving, compassionate, loving God. God's love and mercy are being perfected when we love one another (1 Jn 4:12). To show love and mercy is to let God's love and mercy be unveiled. God's greatest perfection among all His other deeds is found most manifested when we show merciful love to others.

AN INVOLVING LOVE

As you touch more intimately God as immediately present and indwelling within your very being, the more intimately are you also drawn to a union of love toward your neighbor. St. Dorotheus of the 6th century used the example of a wheel. The closer the spokes of the wheel moved to the center, the closer they came to each other. The farther they moved out from center, the more distance separated one spoke from another.

We think of how God's involving love and mercy are manifested in the bent-over figure of a Mother Teresa of Calcutta as she brings God's healing love to the sick and dying of India. Archbishop Oscar Romero of San Salvador was martyred on March 24, 1980. He gave his life for his faith in God and his love for his people who were oppressed by the ruling powers in his country of El Salvador. He moved beyond speech to action. He abandoned all security and lived in constant risk as he involved himself more and more in the sufferings and oppressions of the landless poor. Knowing that his stands against the rich were precipitating him toward a violent death, he spoke in one of his last sermons: "I have tried to sow hope, to maintain hope among the people. There is a liberating Christ who has the strength to save us. I try to give my people this hope.... If I am killed, I will rise in the Salvadorean people."

Today more than ever with the communication media allowing us to be "present" to billions of people around the world, no Christian can not but be concerned with the rampant poverty, physical, psychic and spiritual, that covers most human beings like a suffocating black cloud. We cannot muffle our ears and black out the cries of our suffering brothers and sisters, wherever in the world they may be victims of oppression, wars or natural calamities. Dr. Albert Schweitzer said repeatedly that as long as there was a single person in the world who was hungry, sick, lonely or living in fear, that person was his own responsibility. He truly shows us an example of a human person who released the loving mercy of God into this world in his own human involvement with the suffering ones in Africa.

This is ultimately the true test of our Christianity and of how humanly mature we are: the degree of our involvement in bringing mercy and love to those suffering.

> 'For I was hungry and you gave me food; I was thirsty and you gave me drink; I was a stranger and you made me welcome; naked and you clothed me, sick and you visited me, in prison and you came to see me.' Then the virtuous will say to him in reply, 'Lord, when did we see you hungry and feed you; or thirsty and give you drink? When did we see you a stranger and make you welcome; naked and clothe you; sick or in prison and go to see you?' And the King will answer, 'I tell you solemnly, insofar as you did this to one of the least of these brothers of mine, you did it to me' (Mt 25:35-40).

You and I know that our faith in God's love for us and our "affective" return of that love to God by words alone are dead without an effective involvement in manifesting unselfish love to others in need. "If one of the brothers or one of the sisters is in need of clothes and has not enough food to live on, and one of you says to them, 'I wish you well, keep yourself warm and eat plenty,' without giving them these bare necessities of life, then what good is that? Faith is like that; if good works do not go with it, it is quite dead" (Jm 2:15-17).

A LOVING CONCERN

Through your deep, involving love shown toward one other person, be it God or a friend, you come to learn that true love cannot be turned inward in an exclusive way: it breaks out toward a larger community where you find your love growing as you assume responsibility for the happiness of your brothers and sisters. If your prayer is authentic and deeply transforming, if you truly are living in the presence of God's intimate, unselfish love for you, you will be turned toward others, especially those who have the greatest need, physically, psychically and spiritually.

Yet how you will release God's love as an intimately concerned God for His children will depend greatly on your talents and state of life. But openness to the world community is the sign of love as a growing process of your leading others to find their true identity as beautiful, worthwhile persons.

We lose our credibility as Christians if we go to prayer before God and do not return more humble and more joyfully concerned with the anguish and sufferings of our neighbors around us. We need to allow the anguished cry for justice that rises from suffering human beings around the world first to arise from the depths of our being as we struggle with their burdens and realize that their lot is ours, that their sufferings are our sufferings. What affects others must affect us deeply.

The Gospel is not primarily a blueprint for overcoming social injustices in order to bring about a world of equality for all. Yet Christians who are called to live the Gospel of Jesus

Christ are impelled by the inner presence of God's indwelling love to enter the political, social and economic arenas and there to become a prophetic witness to God's promises of justice, peace and universal brotherhood. A Cesar Chavez, an Archbishop Romero, a Dorothy Day and a Mother Teresa of Calcutta will witness to the Good News of Jesus Christ and will release His intimate love for all mankind in ways different from the forms of witness of a Christian teacher in grade school, a housewife, a diocesan priest or a nurse in a hospital.

A RECONCILER

As the love of God takes over progressively more and more in your conscious awareness that He is the inner Center empowering you to go forth in God's own power of self-sacrificing love toward others, you move horizontally toward others. You become a tender, loving, concerned person in their needs, be they extrinsic, psychic or spiritual. You wish to share with others the love, peace and joy that you abundantly and habitually receive from God in prayer. You become more aware that you are called in every life situation to be an instrument of peace, to become a reconciler of people living in disharmony with themselves, with God and with the world around them. "And all things are of God who has reconciled us to himself by Jesus Christ and has given to us the ministry of reconciliation" (2 Cor 5:18).

There are no strangers for you, but only brothers and sisters. And when you anguish as to what you can do more to release God's great love within your heart, you find the call to stand between your suffering brothers and sisters and God and with outstretched arms you humbly offer the high-priestly prayer of Christ to His Father that they all may be one as He and the Father are one (Jn 17:22-23).

PASCHAL VICTORY

The Good News of Christianity is that God as community abides within us in total, intimate self-giving. We are transformed by this divine, loving presence into unique persons aware that we live in eternity even now. Still we live also in time, the broken time in our broken spatial existence that is in warring contrast against the eternal life given to us by God, the way that darkness assaults the first rays of daylight.

Daily we are faced with this tensioned living between the *already* of Christ's victory over sin and death, and the *not yet* of our continued brokenness along with that of the world around us that groans with us in agonizing pain before we can all come into the fullness of God's love (Rm 8:22).

Yet always we live in the paschal hope that through Jesus Christ's resurrectional victory, all human beings are now capable of sharing in His glorious, eternal life by the forgiveness of their sins and their living in the unity of the love of the Spirit. We breathe confidence, not in our own power to effect change in the world around us, but because of the faith-experience of Christ's risen presence, living within us and sharing with us His eternal life with His Heavenly Father in His unifying Spirit of love.

THE INNER LIGHT

The indwelling Trinity shines like brilliant rays from the sun within you. God's light is within you, even though you still possess a share of the world's darkness. In peaceful joy you move in the power of that loving light into God's created world. Because you have stretched out and yielded constantly to God's inner, indwelling presence, you can now go forth in child-like hope to see God's glory shining from all corners of creation. It is a soft, almost dim, dawn-like shadow of what could burst forth into the blaze of high noon. You intuit by the Spirit's faith, hope and love what most other human beings fail to see. You surrender your child-like weaknesses to God's omnipotent power, to allow His love to pour over you and empower you to go forward to let His love touch those whom you touch.

LIVING IN LOVE

The presence of God within you becomes a swelling ocean wave that seeks to burst through the space of your heart to flow out and inundate the entire world before you with God's love. You whisper the name and presence of Father, Son and Holy Spirit over your world. What was hidden now becomes revealed, what was absent now through your cooperation becomes present.

The presence of God experienced as intimate love within you becomes a presence of God as transforming love around you. You are called to intimacy by living in the indwelling presence of God. But such intimacy finds its fullness in the *birthing* of God's loving presence in others to whom you are sent to serve with love.

Intimate love begets other intimate loves. A loving community gives birth to new loving communities. And you find your happiness and fulfillment, as God does, in becoming progressively more open and available to beget others into their unique happiness as they discover their *I-ness* in the *Thou* of your gift of self.

That is why the archetype of the Church and of us Christians from earliest centuries has always been Mary, virgin and mother of God. It is not enough to realize in prayer throughout the day and night that you have been chosen by God's predilection to be His spouse, a pure and empty virgin with no power but the power of awe-ful expectancy to receive the triune God's gift of indwelling, intimate love. Caught in loving ecstasy, you turn within and surrender your whole being in obedient submission to the indwelling Trinity. "My Beloved is mine and I am his" (Sg 2:16).

You are called to be mother of the God life in the world around you. Yet how can you birth God into being in the lives of others unless you have first virginally surrendered to His intimate presence within you?

The words of Meister Eckhart, the 14th century Rhenish mystic of the Dominican Order, can fittingly conclude this book on God's call to all of us to live in intimacy in His indwelling presence which can reach its fruition only in bringing to life, as a mother does, God's intimate presence in the lives of others. For therein lies our individual fulfillment which partakes of the cosmic fulfillment of all things in God and God in all things.

> For man to become fruitful, he must become a woman. Woman! That is the most noble word that can be addressed to the soul, and it is far nobler than virgin. That man should conceive God within himself is good and in this predisposition he is a virgin. But that God should become fruitful in him is better. For to become fruitful through the gift received is to be grateful for the gift. And then the intellect becomes a woman in its gratitude that conceives anew.

Following Jesus in the Real World:
ASCETICISM TODAY
Rev. George A. Maloney, SJ

Unfortunately asceticism and mysticism are words which have frightened people to the extent that they have been unwilling to inquire what they could mean in their lives. Father Maloney explains and establishes practical applications for those who would lead others to the way of perfection and for those who individually seek to apply the principles to their own lives.

Cassette 1: What Is Asceticism? Christian Perfection, Asceticism of Prayer, Reflective Healing, Cultic Asceticism, Problems of Asceticism, Jesus Christ—the Ascetic, Faith Asceticism, Asceticism of the Cross, Asceticism for the Modern Christian, Asceticism of Work, Social Asceticism, Asceticism Leads to Contemplation

Cassette 2: Pastoral Orientation, Psychology and Mortification, Areas of Discipline, Modern Asceticism, Asceticism of Vows, Conclusion.

TAH093—2 cassettes in dustproof shelf-case—approximately 2 hours—$14.95